My Book of

QUESTIONS

and

ANSWERS

What is a dugong?

Sailors' stories about sighting mermaids playing in the Pacific are probably based on seeing the dugong. The dugong is a gentle, harmless sea mammal which basks in the shallow waters of the Pacific. It is about three metres long and looks like a seal with the head of a walrus. The dugong is closely related to the manatee and sea cow. It never leaves its home in rivers or the sea, where it feeds on grass and weed.

Like the whale, the dugong provides people with meat and oil, and so it has been hunted in great numbers by the aborigines of Australia. Even its tears have been sought and collected because they are supposed to bring good luck. If the hunting of the dugong could be controlled, it might be possible to breed large herds of them such as people do with cattle to provide us with another source of food.

Who wanted King Neptune's Cows?

Long ago the Ancient Romans told stories of King Neptune's wonderful kingdom beneath the sea. Magic cows and horses grazed in lush meadows around his palace.

A fisherman and his wife lived on a small rocky island above Neptune's kingdom. The wife secretly longed for a cow to give them milk, butter and cream. So, one day she sailed out to sea and sang Neptune a song, asking him for a cow. As her song ended, a great storm arose and drove the boat back to land. When the storm died down, a fat cow stood on the island, chewing contentedly.

Soon the fisherwife wanted even more milk, and she sang another song to Neptune, who once again sent her a cow. And so it continued: more songs and more cows until the island was overflowing. To make room for all the cows, the couple decided to make their island bigger by throwing large stones into the sea. But the stones landed on Neptune's head and he grew very angry. He rose out of the sea and punished the greedy woman by taking back all the magic cows.

Why were the pirates feared?

Pirates flew their own flag, called the Jolly Roger, from the main top-mast of their ships. They took the name from the French Buccaneers' red flag, called *le joli rouge,* which is French for the pretty red one. It was hoisted just as they sighted their enemy. The pirate crew gave a brave cheer as it unfurled. They knew how frightened other sailors would be, when they saw the dreaded skull and crossbones. Often ships surrendered immediately at the sight of the flag.

Sometimes pirates played cunning tricks on their enemies. Instead of flying the Jolly Roger, they flew the same flag as the enemy ship. The captain of a Spanish galleon would not be alarmed if he saw a ship sailing towards him, flying a Spanish flag. By the time he realized it was a pirate ship in disguise, it was too late.

Once the pirates had surrounded a ship, they boarded it. They swung ropes up over the sides of the ship. These ropes, with hooks on the ends, were called creepers.

The pirates swarmed up, carrying weapons in their mouths or tucked firmly into their belts. They carried pistols and many different kinds of knives. The cutlass was a broad flat sword with a sharp curved blade, designed for slashing and cutting. Long, slender swords such as the rapier were used to fight duels. Pirates tucked smaller knives into their belts, and pulled them out in a flash.

How do people count?

People first used to count on their fingers and thumbs. This is why we use the numbers 1 to 10 when we count. The earliest counting machine, or computer, was an abacus. It was first used in China some 5,000 years ago. If we want to count out a pile of beads, we group them in UNITS, TENS and HUNDREDS. On the abacus the beads are placed on wires. Ten beads in the UNITS column can be replaced by one bead in the TENS column. Ten beads in that column can be replaced by one bead in the HUNDREDS column. The abacus helps us to count, and stores the total until we need it. Can you read these numbers on the abacus?

A computer works so quickly and efficiently that it seems to have magical powers! In fact it is a machine that only does what it is told to do. The instructions it is given must always be simple, such as, 'Add these two numbers.' The computer follows thousands of instructions in one second, and can solve all sorts of difficult problems. How long does it take you to work out this calculation:

$$426 + 92 + 3312 - 447 + 381 - 555 - 91 + 442 + 11 - 6$$

Imagine how long it might take you to work out a difficult calculation such as the one on the blackboard:

You would soon grow tired if you had to spend the entire day working out such sums. You might make mistakes and would certainly become very bored. You could spend all your life doing work that a computer would finish in a few seconds.

Where do magical people live?

For centuries, people believed that small magical people shared their homes and countryside. These small, elf-like people were teasing and mischievous. They were often blamed for accidents, for making startling noises and for causing frights and surprises. The tiny people are described differently in almost every country of the world.

Irish leprechauns are said to wear green clothes. Like pixies, elves and imps, they play tricks on humans. They may blow out candles on dark stairs, make frightening noises in walls or lead travellers astray across bogs and moors.

The bunyip is a legendary water monster, half reptile and half mammal, that lurks in the muddy waterholes and lagoons of the Australian outback. It lures its victims into the dark water with its glowing eyes. On moonlight nights it sometimes rises to the surface and utters bloodcurdling moans, warning all creatures to keep away.

Giants were supposed to be huge magical people, blamed for rock falls, floods and wild storms. In Northern Ireland, six-sided rocks have been thrown up by the volcanic eruptions below the Earth's surface. The rocks lie neatly arranged in steps. The people who lived there believed that a group of giants had once built these, and so they called the steps the Giant's Causeway.

What food comes from the sea?

The sea contains riches which are becoming more valuable to us as supplies of food and fuel grow scarcer on land. Many sea creatures and plants, which are good to eat, can be farmed along the seashore.

When the tide goes out, shells are left stranded in tidal pools, scattered over the beach or clinging to rocks. Molluscs are soft, boneless creatures that often live inside a hard shell for protection. Some molluscs are spiral shaped like snail shells, whelks and winkles and others are bivalves and have two parts joined together by a hinge, like a mussel or clam.

Many molluscs are good to eat. People collect winkles, whelks and mussels and scoop the soft creature out of the shell to eat. Other molluscs such as clams and cockles bury themselves in the sand. At low tide people use rakes to dig them up. Clams, mussels and oysters are farmed or grown in special areas of shallow water called beds.

Another group of sea creatures which have hard outer shells are called crustaceans. Shrimps, lobsters and crabs are all crustaceans. Their tough shells are jointed like suits of armour so that the creatures can swim and crawl easily As the animal inside grows, the shell splits off and is replaced by a new, larger one. Many crustaceans are delicious to eat and are caught in traps or nets. In North America lobsters are raised from eggs in hatcheries.

Who saved Androcles?

Androcles was a Roman slave who worked for a cruel master. One day he ran away and managed to avoid being captured by the Roman soldiers who were sent to catch him. After a tiring journey, he crawled into a dark cave and fell asleep.

A fierce roar woke him. Filling the entrance of the cave, he saw a huge, shaggy lion with flashing eyes. Androcles trembled with fear for he knew he could not escape.

He was astonished when, instead of leaping on him, the lion limped forward in pain, lay down on its side and licked its wounded paw. Androcles saw a large thorn sticking into the fleshy pad. Without flinching, he knelt by the lion and carefully pulled out the thorn. The lion showed its gratitude by not harming Androcles.

But one day Androcles was captured by a patrol of Roman soldiers, who recognized him as a runaway slave. They took him before the Emperor, who decided his punishment.

'I will throw you to the lions,' he shouted.

On a day of the Games, Androcles was led into the great amphitheatre. The excited crowds cheered as the cage gates opened and several lions leapt out. They approached Androcles, snarling greedily. Suddenly one lion rushed ahead of the others and pushed Androcles to the ground. It stood over him protectively, growling and clawing at the other beasts when they came near. The lion was Androcles' old friend, who was now able to repay his good deed.

The crowd had never seen such a sight. They cheered Androcles and begged the Emperor to set him free. The Emperor raised his thumbs and Androcles was led from the arena, a free man.

How is oil drilled?

A drill pipe is sunk deep into the seabed, more pipes being added to lengthen it, and make a long, watertight tube.

   At the bottom tip of the tube the drill bit spins around at a tremendous speed, gouging out a circular hole in the rock of the seabed, about the size of a dinner plate. It is called the borehole.

The drill bit is made from hard steel which is shaped into powerful metal teeth. These wear down very quickly, so they are studded with industrial diamonds for extra strength. Diamonds are harder than rock, so they do not wear down during drilling. They are not the diamonds set in jewellery, but have been specially cut, heated and dipped in chemicals.

The bit gets hot as it drills. It is cooled by a muddy mixture of chemicals pumped inside the watertight tube. This 'mud' carries away the loose rock chippings and keeps the hole free of rubble.

As the 'mud' flows back up the tube, it passes through a filter. All the rock pieces are cleaned out, and the pure 'mud' travels back up to the top of the pipe, ready to flow down the tube again.

Scientists on the oil rig examine the 'mud' carefully, looking for loose chippings containing drops of oil. If the 'mud' is frothy with tiny bubbles or trapped air or gas it might be that the drill has struck oil, as gas and oil are often found together.

When the bit pierces the spongy rock that contains oil, the gassy air fizzes up the borehole in a great spurt, bringing the oil with it. After millions of years the gas and oil have found a way to escape.

But the thick 'mud', moving up and down the pipe, traps the escaping oil. A great tap, called a valve, is fitted over the drill hole. The oil flow can now be turned on and off like running water.

The many pipes and valves, spread all over the oilfield, are nicknamed Christmas trees.

Who were the first Red Indians?

In 1492 Christopher Columbus set sail westward from Portugal to find a new route to India. Instead, he discovered the continent of North America, which was inhabited by natives with reddish copper skins. Thinking he had reached India, Columbus called these people Indians.

There were many different Indian peoples, each with their own language, customs and way of life. The most well-known were the Plains Indians who roamed the grassy plains of North America. The men hunted buffalo with bows and arrows, or axes called tomahawks. They used the buffalo skins for clothing and for their tents, called tepees.

They ate the meat. They carved the horns into utensils and used the hair for mattresses.

The women worked in the villages. They harvested crops of maize and beans and ground them into flour. They gathered wild berries and roots for food. The mothers carried their babies, called papooses, strapped to their backs.

The Indians believed in guardian spirits that protected them, and brought them good harvests and victory in battle. The spirits took the shapes of animals, birds, trees, mountains, rivers and even flashes of lightning. Each tribe had its own spirit. The Indians decorated their tepees, rugs and clothes with pictures of these spirits. Some tribes carved them on totem poles, which they stood in the centre of their villages.

As the European settlers spread, they pushed the Indians further and further west. Even then, the cattle ranchers, buffalo hunters and the transcontinental railroad invaded the Indians' last territory. The Indians fought fiercely to protect their land and way of life. After many battles the United States Cavalry finally defeated them. The remaining Indians were forced to change their ways. Some adopted the American way of life. Others chose to live in special camps, called reservations, where they have little freedom.

Which President named a toy?

Theodore Roosevelt, who was nicknamed Teddy, was a president of the United States of America. In 1903, while on a hunting trip to Mississippi, a small bear cub crossed his path. Teddy refused to shoot it. Later, a cartoon was published in an American newspaper, showing the President and his small animal friend.

Soon afterwards, a toy maker wrote to President Roosevelt asking if he could produce a soft, cuddly toy called Teddy's Bear. The toy was an instant success and today, almost every child has a lop-eared, much-worn and cuddled teddy bear.

Which Prime Minister played with toy soldiers?

Until the twentieth century, generals drew up their battle lines as if they were playing with lines of toy soldiers. The soldiers were placed in key positions, and when the order to charge was given, each unit knew where to move. The tiny tin or lead soldiers of a hundred years ago were painted with uniforms of different battalions and even the details of their bayonets or swords were accurate. They were hollow soldiers standing three centimetres high, and often formed very valuable collections.

Sir Winston Churchill, the famous British Prime Minister, helped to lead Britain to victory in the Second World War. As a young boy he often played with toy soldiers, lining them up in ranks and organizing very efficient battles. His father was impressed and suggested to Winston that he should join the army, where he could direct real soldiers rather than toy ones.

How did the mouse save the lion?

Over two thousand years ago, a slave called Aesop entertained his Greek masters with tales of animals and birds. Each tale, or fable, contained a hidden meaning which gave advice or a warning to the listener. His fable of the Lion and the Mouse shows how an act of kindness to someone else will often be repaid unexpectedly.

A lion was sleeping in his lair when a tiny mouse accidentally ran across his nose and woke him up. The lion was furious and trapped the mouse under his paw, ready to kill him.

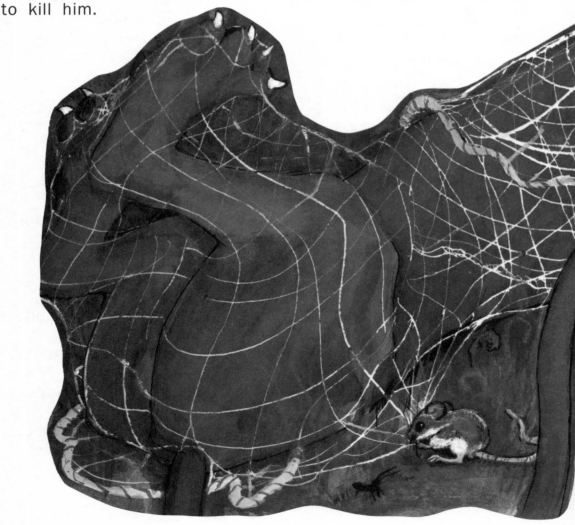

But the little mouse was so apologetic and humble that the lion grew generous and released him.
'After all,' he thought, 'what good would it do me to kill this small, harmless thing. It wouldn't even make a good meal.'

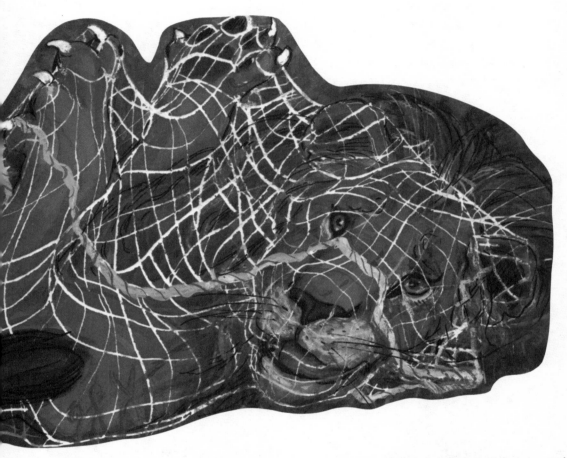

Not long afterwards, the lion was hunting in the woods when he became tangled in a net that had been laid as a trap by some hunters. The lion struggled frantically, roaring with fear. He knew that the hunters would soon return. The little mouse recognized the roar and ran to see what he could do. His sharp teeth soon gnawed a large hole in the net and the lion was freed.

In the end, it was a tiny, weak creature who saved the life of the king of the beasts.

What is the Lutine Bell?

In 1799 the sailing frigate *La Lutine* set sail from the south coast of England for the German port of Hamburg. It was heavily laden with bars of gold. As it rounded the Dutch coast a violent storm blew up. The ship was wrecked, the crew drowned and all the gold lost. Over the years, divers have recovered only a small part of the sunken gold. However, they have found a cannon, the rudder and some furniture, the captain's watch and the ship's bell.

Today the Lutine Bell hangs in the hall of a large London insurance house called Lloyds. It is rung whenever important announcements are to be made. Two strokes announce good news, and one stroke, bad news.
On 29 December 1975, the Lutine Bell was rung once when the enormous oil tanker the *Berge Istra* sank, and all but two of the crew were drowned.

What is a bathyscaphe?

At the edge of the Continental Shelf, the land plunges steeply. In some places it drops several kilometres to the ocean floor. Like the surface of the Earth, the ocean floor rises and falls in huge mountains and deep trenches. No sunlight ever reaches this far down, so it is very cold. Strange creatures live in the depths that never rise to the warmer waters above.

In 1930 two scientists invented a special submarine called a bathysphere to explore these great depths. It was a ball large enough for a person to crouch inside and contained its own air supply. The only difficulty was that it had to be lowered from a ship by a steel cable. A few years later Auguste Piccard invented an improved deep water submarine called the bathyscaphe. It works like a hot air balloon in reverse. To go down, the diver attaches weights to the bathyscaphe, and to rise to the surface the diver releases the weights. In the bathyscaphe the scientist can explore creatures in the ocean depths and collect samples of rock from the seabed.

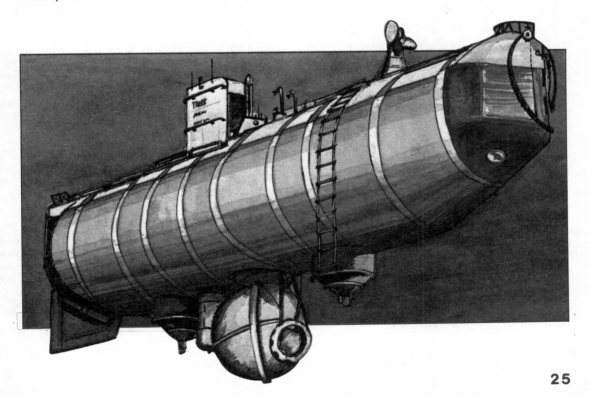

Why do animals become extinct?

The dodo, a large clumsy bird which could not fly, used to live on the island of Mauritius near Africa. But European settlers changed the dodo's habitat and took away its supply of food. By 1681, there were no living dodos. It was extinct. Many other kinds of animals and birds have become extinct in recent years. There are many more that soon might only exist as stuffed creatures in a museum.

A few years ago a group of scientists collected information about hundreds of animals and birds which are in danger of dying out. They published their findings in the Red Data Book.

The Red Data Book tries to make people aware of the need to protect all living things. It warns that animals that are hunted for their skins and fur, such as the tiger and the polar bear, or for their meat and fatty oils, such as the whale, will soon die out completely.

How does a fire start?

On a cold, wintry day you rub your hands together briskly to make them warm. Long ago, cavemen rubbed two dry sticks together very fast. The sticks grew warm and started to smoulder. The cavemen blew on the smouldering wood and made a flame.

Another way to light a fire is by using sparks. When a hammer hits a nail, sometimes sparks shoot out. Cavemen made sparks by striking a piece of flint against a lump of hard rock. They held some dried grass or tree bark to the sparks and set it alight. Thousands of years later men were still using this method. They put flint and steel in a tinder box to light rags.

Today we use safety matches, which is a much easier and safer way to light a fire. The ends of small strips of wood, usually pinewood, are dipped in chemicals. They burst into flame when struck against the rough surface on a matchbox.

Outdoor fires often start from a carelessly dropped match or a campfire which gets out of control. Dry grass burns easily. The wind sets the undergrowth ablaze and carries sparks to the trees. Acres of forest and woodland are destroyed.

Special signs at the side of the road warn people of fire hazards and tell them how to prevent fires. The code reminds campers to build safe fires. Fires must be extinguished with water or buried under earth or sand.

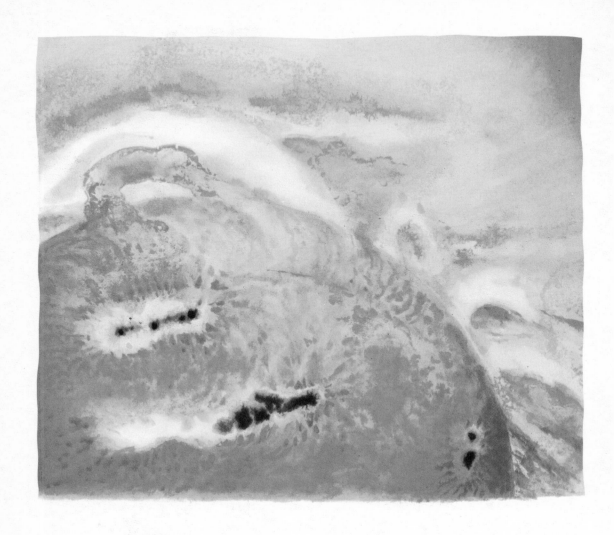

What is the sun made of?

The sun is a ball of exploding gases. Nobody can travel to the sun because the terrific heat would burn them to a cinder. The temperature near the sun is thousands of times hotter than boiling water. The surface of the sun is about 6,000° C and its centre is close to 14,000,000° C!

If the heat of the sun were to alter even slightly, we would notice great changes on Earth. A little more heat would make the Earth unbearably hot to live on. A little less heat would cause the oceans to freeze.

Astronomers watch the changes that take place on the sun's surface. Sometimes they see sunspots which are dark patches among the burning gases. They appear as huge, ragged holes in the sun's surface. It is difficult to say why they are there, or why they vanish after a short time.

Sometimes, great flares burst from the sunspots, hurling small dust particles into space. These particles make beautiful displays of colour which light the sky over the most northern and most southern countries of the world. The northern lights are called the Aurora Borealis. The lights in the south are called the Aurora Australis.

Who was Merlin?

Storytellers have been writing about Arthur, Guinevere and the Knights of the Round Table since the Dark Ages well over one thousand years ago. Arthur's adviser was the powerful wizard Merlin.

There was a tradition that whoever pulled the magic sword out of a great stone would be king. When all the other knights had failed, Arthur removed the sword with the aid of Merlin's magic, to become King of England and Wales.

Legend says that Merlin placed Stonehenge where it stands today. Arthur's father, King Uther, wished to honour the burial ground of his knights killed in battle. Merlin sailed to Ireland to find the Giant's Ring, a huge circle of tall standing stones. Using his magic, he collapsed the stones, lifted them on board his ship, and set them up again on Salisbury Plain in the south of England.

What are fairy rings?

In fairy tales, fairies reward people who are good and generous. A woman who places a saucer of milk on her doorstep will find her housework done in the morning. Children who bravely pull out wobbly teeth will find that the fairies have placed a silver coin under their pillows when they wake in the morning.

Superstitious people say that a circle of worn grass or a ring of mushrooms marks the spot where fairies dance at their midnight revels. They warn you not to step inside the ring as you might be pinched black and blue or be carried off to fairyland. Spiteful fairies may exchange their elfin babies for human children. Without knowing it, the human mothers rear these changelings, until one day they suddenly notice their children have pointed ears and tiny sprouting wings!

Where did a volcano grow in a farmer's field?

One morning, Dionisio Pulido was at work on his small farm close to the little village of Paricutin in Mexico. He worked hard, pushing the plough up and down the field. The warm sun beat down on his bare arms and chest, but strangely it was Dionisio's feet that were feeling unusually hot. As he examined the ground, he heard a deep rumble coming from the soil. Suddenly the earth shook violently and a great hole opened up before him. Smoke and dust hissed and whistled from the hole.

Dionisio was terrified. He fled to the village to find help.

Steam and gas continued to escape from the hole throughout the day. That night glowing rocks and cinders lit the sky. By the next morning, Dionisio's field was buried under a huge cone-shaped mountain which grew larger every hour. Soon lava started to flow out from the centre of the mountain, and buried the farm and the neighbouring village.

The volcano Paricutin was born.

Which plants and animals can survive in the desert?

In many parts of the world, enough rain falls to fill the lakes, reservoirs, rivers and streams. The sun dries up some of the water, but soon the winds blow cool air from the sea. Clouds form in the chilly air and rain falls again. But in the hottest countries, the sun shines fiercely almost every day. The intense heat dries up all the dampness in the soil. Even the winds are warm and dry, so they do not help to make clouds.

It is not easy to stay alive in the desert. There are few streams and pools to provide water for thirsty animals or crops. The plants and creatures that survive in the desert have had to adapt their lives to the dryness.

Plants such as the cactus and the gum tree store water in their thick, prickly stems, or in rubbery, waxy leaves. Animals and birds shelter during the hottest hours of the day. They hunt for food either when the sun is low in the sky or at night. Some animals, such as the jack rabbit, burrow deep into the earth to stay cool. When a camel gets thirsty, it chews the spiky cactus leaves that are full of water. It can live for many days on water and fat stored in its hump.

What is oil used for?

Oil is needed to keep the modern world running smoothly. It is surprising how many things need oil to make them run and to keep them in good working order.

Most engines need oil to power them, others need oil to grease their wheels and make them spin smoothly without friction.

Many different companies are drilling for oil on land and sea. They turn this oil into petrol, and deliver it by tankers to all the petrol stations.

Before electricity was discovered, houses were lit by candles made from oil. There were also lamps, which burnt a special oil called paraffin. A long, cotton wick was soaked in paraffin and set alight. It gave out a bright but smoky glow. The wick in an oil heater glows in the same way.

Oil is necessary to make electric power. In power stations it is burnt to make steam. Huge steam turbine engines whirr into action and make electricity. The electricity runs along heavy cables to light and heat our homes. Electricity also operates machines in factories.

Many toys are made of plastic. Plastic is made by mixing oil and chemicals together. Materials made in this way are called synthetic fabrics. Nylon, polythene and p.v.c. are synthetic fabrics. Clothes, bedclothes, carpets, curtains and even cushions are probably all made from synthetic fabrics. Paint on doors and walls may contain oil. Many soaps or medicines also have oil in them.

Where did the pirates attack?

The Mediterranean was the busiest route for ships carrying goods between countries in the East and those in the West. For hundreds of years Moorish pirates from the coast of North Africa ruled the Mediterranean.

The fiercest Moors were known as the Barbary Corsairs. Most of them had a different religion from other peoples living around the Mediterranean. They were Moslems. Moslems and Christians hated each other. When Moslems captured enemy ships, they made slaves of the Christian sailors.

Many countries sent ships to defeat the Barbary Corsairs. But the Corsairs were rich and powerful and owned a fleet of thousands of ships. They nearly always defeated their enemies and escaped capture.

Countries in the East had silks and spices which Europe wanted.

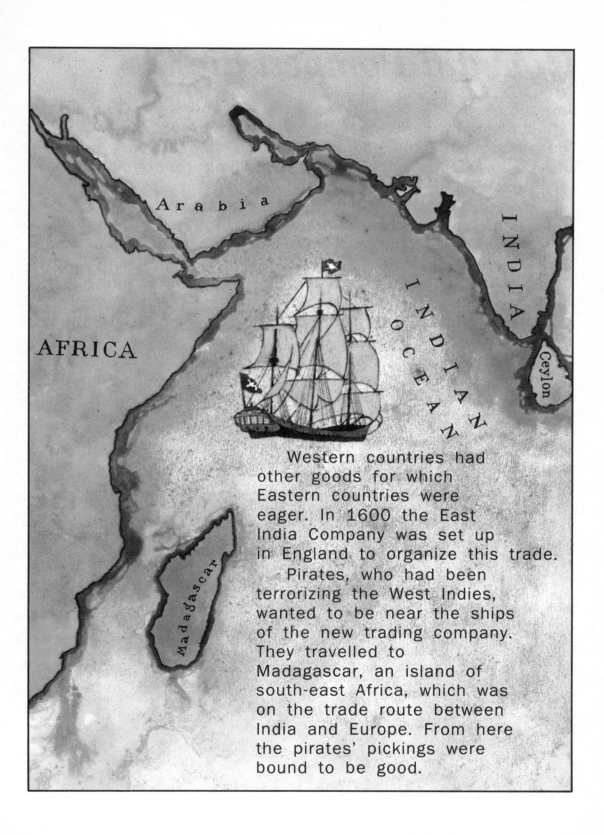

Arabia

AFRICA

INDIA

INDIAN OCEAN

Ceylon

Madagascar

Western countries had other goods for which Eastern countries were eager. In 1600 the East India Company was set up in England to organize this trade.

Pirates, who had been terrorizing the West Indies, wanted to be near the ships of the new trading company. They travelled to Madagascar, an island of south-east Africa, which was on the trade route between India and Europe. From here the pirates' pickings were bound to be good.

How did Pompeii die?

Sometimes people who live near a volcano think that it is extinct. Nobody can remember seeing it erupt.
The mountain makes no noise and no smoke pours out.
Life on its slopes and in the surrounding countryside is very peaceful.

Two thousand years ago life was particularly good around the volcano called Vesuvius in Southern Italy.
Rich vineyards and orchards grew on its slopes.
The neighbouring towns of Pompeii and Herculaneum were also wealthy. They had fine temples and market places, and the Roman people built elegant villas in which to live.

Suddenly, quiet Vesuvius erupted. Thick clouds of smoke and poisonous gas poured out, followed by heavy showers of small rocks, dust and ash. Within a short time the town of Pompeii lay buried, and Herculaneum was swallowed by a river of mud. Only a few inhabitants managed to escape.

Both towns remained buried and forgotten until about two hundred years ago, when some Roman remains were dug up accidentally. The ash and rock were cleared away until the towns were discovered. The houses had been preserved under the volcanic dust. So had the bodies of many of the Roman people and their animals. Everyone had been taken by surprise when the volcano erupted. Families sat at dinner and guards stood on duty, just as they had been caught when the lava poured over them. Today the towns of Pompeii and Herculaneum are kept as museums where visitors can see how people lived in Roman times.

Why do you have a shadow?

On a clear sunny day sunlight is all around us.
When clouds pass between the sun and the earth, they
block off some of the light. The earth below is in shadow.

At midday the sun shines down from its highest
position in the sky. The sun's rays fall directly down to the
ground from above. Your shadow will be fat and squat.
In the morning and evening the sun is lower in the sky.
Your shadow will be long and thin.

The shadow thrown by a tree is the shape of a tree.
The shadow thrown by a person is the shape of that
person.

In the shade it is cooler and darker than in the sunlight. Too much strong sunlight can be harmful. Sunbathers sit behind beach umbrellas to protect themselves from the powerful rays of the sun. Panting dogs stretch out in the shade of a cool spot. Insects shelter in the shade of petals and leaves.

Why does rain fall?

When the air grows cooler, the water vapour begins to cool, too. The water drops hang together in big, fluffy clouds high in the air.
   When the clouds grow too heavy with water drops, it begins to rain. The drops fall to the ground and gather in puddles. After the rain clouds pass, the sun may come out. The heat of the sun warms the ground and dries up the puddles. Each little drop of water becomes tinier and lighter. The heat turns the water into a gas called water vapour. This rises into the air, and the cycle repeats all over again.

Which is your birth sign?

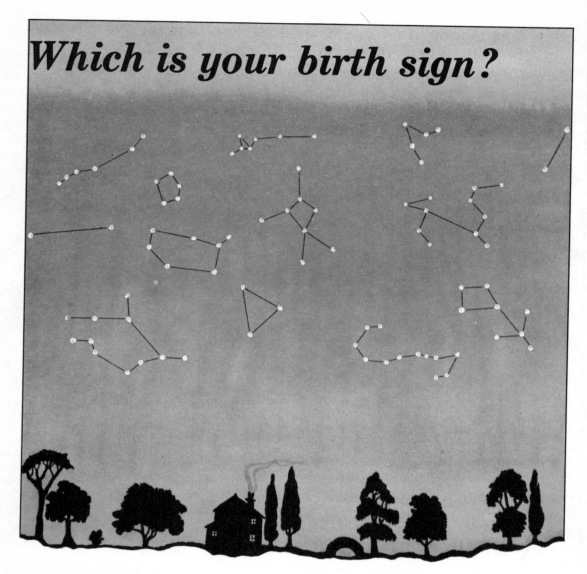

For thousands of years, people looking at the night sky have seen patterns in the stars. Astrologers believe that these patterns hold a message. They have named the belt of stars that lie in the sun's path, the Zodiac. The belt is divided into twelve sections and each section has a Zodiac sign and name.

Astrologers believe that the positions of the stars and planets at a person's birth can explain their character. If you want to know about your personality, you must give the astrologer the date, place and exact time of your birth.

Which is your Zodiac sign? What can you find out about people who are born under your sign?

If your birthday falls between the third week of July and the third week of August you were born under the Zodiac sign of Leo. Leo means lion, and people born under this sign are said to be proud, grand, generous and sometimes boastful, just as a lion is.

Over thirty stars form the shape of Leo, although only a few of these shine brightly in the night sky. Each November, showers of falling stars shoot from Leo. These meteorites are called Leonites.

What is seismology?

The surface of the Earth has been changing its shape for millions of years. Far below the ground, the layers of rock that form the Earth's crust, still twist and fold as liquid rock from the Earth's fiery core forces its way through.

Seismology is the study of this shifting movement in the Earth's crust. For example, an instrument called a tiltmeter can record any changes in the level of the ground surrounding a volcano. A volcano's vent sometimes grows wider as hot lava pushes its way upwards, so scientists can predict an eruption long before it happens and warn people who live nearby of the coming danger.

When looking for oil at sea, scientists gather samples and make many tests. Dynamite is fired into the sea, where there may be an oilfield. Soon the thundering roar of the explosion echoes back from below the water. The geologists watch instruments called seismographs. Wavy lines crossing the screen show the echoes as they hit the seabed and pass through layers of hard and soft rock. These lines tell the geologists whether there is oil in the layers of rock.

How does a caterpillar grow into a butterfly?

Red Admiral butterflies live in North America and along the shores of the Mediterranean Sea. Every year the butterflies travel north to colder countries such as Canada and Britain to lay their eggs.

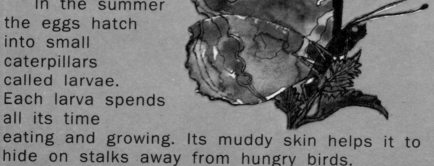

The female lays her eggs on nettle leaves, wraps the leaf carefully over the eggs and fastens it with a silken thread.

In the summer the eggs hatch into small caterpillars called larvae. Each larva spends all its time eating and growing. Its muddy skin helps it to hide on stalks away from hungry birds.

When the larva is several weeks old, it spins itself a silky shell or cocoon covered with gold or silver spots. It attaches this to a leaf or stalk. It is now called a chrysalis. Although the chrysalis does not move, changes are taking place inside the cocoon. The mouth becomes a long feeler with a sucker at the end, wings sprout from its back, its back legs disappear and its front legs grow long.

In late July the chrysalis bursts open. A Red Admiral flies out on black and red wings fluttering among flowers and rotting fruit.

Although some Red Admirals
hibernate during
the winter
months, most of them die.

Who flew too near the Sun?

A famous ancient Greek legend tells the story of Daedalus and his son Icarus, imprisoned in a dark maze on the island of Crete. Carefully, they planned their escape. To flee from the island they had to cross the Mediterranean Sea, which surrounded it. But they had no boat.

Daedalus thought up a clever plan. He and Icarus collected feathers, which they stuck together with wax and strong thread. Daedalus then set to work to model two pairs of huge wings.

They managed to escape out onto a high hill. They strapped the wings onto their arms, and flapped them up and down as if they were huge birds. At last, they soared high into the sky. Soon they left the island behind them and flew out over the sea.

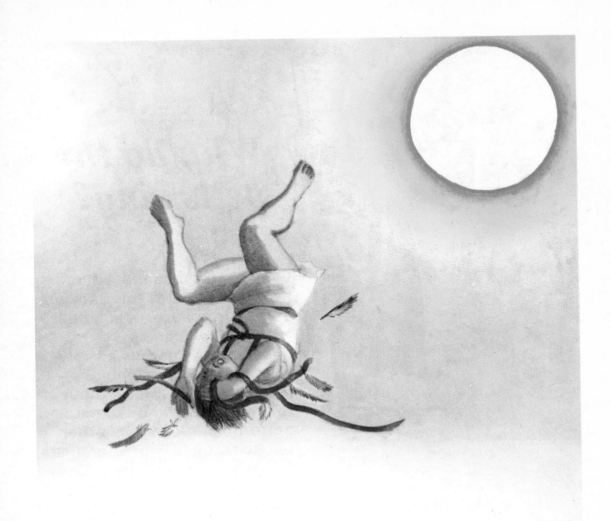

Daedalus called out to Icarus,
'Take care my son! Beware of flying too high!
The wax, holding your feathers together, might
easily melt in the heat of the sun.'
But Icarus was too excited to listen. Soon the wax
softened in the sunshine, and one by one the feathers
dropped from his wings, until Icarus plunged into the sea
and drowned.

Why do the bells ring?

Over four thousand years ago the peoples of Babylon and China were using bells as warning signals, decorations or musical instruments. In some religions, bells were thought to be sacred and able to perform miracles. In other religions bells were, and still are, used to call people to worship.

The oldest bells ever found were unearthed in an Egyptian tomb where they were put to drive away the evil spirits. In Ancient Egypt pregnant women wore necklaces of silver and gold bells to protect their unborn babies.

Today we use bells on all kinds of occasions to attract people's attention. Before newspapers, radio and television carried reports of important events, a town crier patrolled the streets. He rang a bell to get people's attention, and called out the daily news. To warn people of fire, church bells were rung up the scale instead of down. Lookouts, watching from the church tower, were warned of an invasion when they saw beacons flaring on the hills, or heard the distant sound of bells from a neighbouring village. An urgent peal from the belfry warned local inhabitants to rush for their weapons.

Napoleon, Emperor of France, had conquered the city of Moscow and declared himself ruler of Russia. But he had little to celebrate. A large part of the city was burnt to the ground, his troops were starving and the freezing Russian winter had set in. Wearily, he gave the order to start the long march home. As the tired French army set out across the snow-covered plains, the grateful people of Moscow rejoiced. From every tower, bells rang out carrying the happy news to the villages far and wide.

Tchaikovsky, the famous Russian composer, celebrated this victory in a triumphant piece of music. It is called the 1812 Overture, and the final passage is filled with a joyous peal of bells.

What was the Kraken?

Although people have travelled far in sailing ships, rowing boats and on rafts for thousands of years, they knew little about the ocean's depths until recently. Tales of terrifying sea monsters convinced many people that they were safer on land. One story told of a giant octopus called the Kraken, which dragged ships down into the depths with its great tentacles.

However, today people are exploring the undersea world just as they are exploring outer space. Scientists are developing new equipment for diving and exploration and for helping people to live and work underwater.

How can a vacuum cleaner suck up gold?

Scattered over the seabed are large lumps of rock which contain valuable metals such as gold, iron, tin or platinum. These rocks are called mineral nodules.

There are plans to gather these underwater metals by sucking them up from the seabed through long tubes like huge vacuum cleaners. The tubes would be lowered and operated from ships on the surface. Barges would carry the loads of mineral nodules to shore.

Why did Witches keep Familiars?

Wise men and women were sometimes thought to be wizards and witches. They seemed to understand the mysteries of nature, the weather and the countryside. They mixed powdered herbs and flowers into medicines to cure sickness. They chanted spells to grant people's wishes, and predicted what was going to happen.

Although people were frightened of witches and wizards, they respected the magical powers. Exaggerated stories described how witches flew through the night sky on broomsticks, or cursed cattle so that they sickened. Witches were even said to make dead people come to life again!

Witches and wizards kept familiars, or animal pets, to help them with their spells or to spy out information. Familiars had magical powers of their own, too. They could talk like humans, make themselves invisible, or turn into grisly shapes to frighten away enemies.

The most common familiars were black cats with shiny coats and glinting eyes. Other familiars were slimy toads, moles, sharp-eyed ferrets, spiders, weasels, rats and mice. Some were birds like the jackdaw and the owl, who were thought to be sly, mean or wise, like their masters.

Strange familiars were made of mixtures of different animals. One might have the head of a lion, the hooves of a goat and the wings of a bird.

Why do fish carry torches?

Fish that live in the ocean depths are strange and ugly. Their bones are thin and papery and they are often covered with warts and spikes. Most of these fish are scavengers. They feed upon the remains of dead plankton and fish which sink to the seabed. Many are cannibal fish and eat each other. They have huge mouths and stomachs and their large eyes search the darkness for prey.

Some of the deep-sea fish carry their own 'torches' to light up the dark sea and attract and dazzle their prey. The shiny tinge to their skins is caused by a substance in their bodies. Other deep-sea fish called anglers capture their prey with fishing lines attached to their bodies.

As fishermen find it harder to catch fish in shallower waters, they are turning to these deep-sea fish. It is more difficult to catch fish in deep waters, but they taste just as good.

Who would like a bite of seaweed?

Much of the seabed is covered with forests of seaweed. Some plants such as the giant kelp grow up to seventy metres in height while other seaweeds can only be seen through a microscope. Seaweed which grows in shallow waters is rich and green from the sun's light. Red and brown seaweeds grow in deeper waters.

People living along rocky coasts gather seaweed at low tide. They boil it and eat it like cabbage or use it to make bread. Sometimes huge harvesting machines pull the seaweed ashore. At the factory a gluey liquid is squeezed from the seaweed. This liquid is used in making sweets, jellies, ice cream and even sausage skins. Some medicines contain seaweed because of its high iodine content. Farmers fertilize their fields with powdered seaweed to help their crops grow.

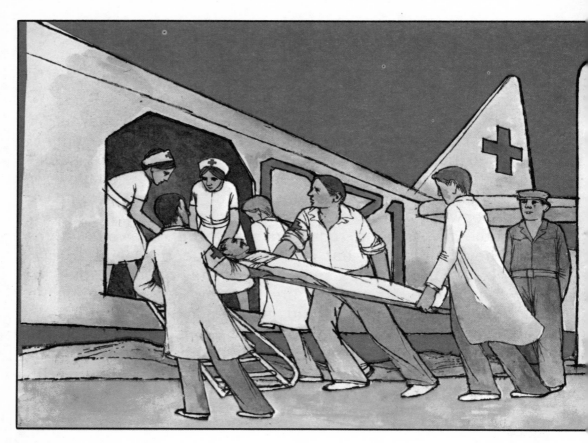

What is the work of the International Red Cross?

After the battle of Solferino in Italy in 1859, soldiers lay dying all over the battlefield. Occasionally an Austrian limped towards his camp, or a Frenchman helped a comrade back to the French side. A few overworked army doctors stooped over the injured and asked stretcher-bearers to carry the soldiers back to the hospital tents.

Most of the injured men received no medical help at all.

Jean-Henri Dunant, a Swiss banker, wrote a stirring report about the horrors he had seen at Solferino. As a result, countries all over the world came together to form the International Red Cross. They set up this organization to care for wounded soldiers. They agreed that in wartime the

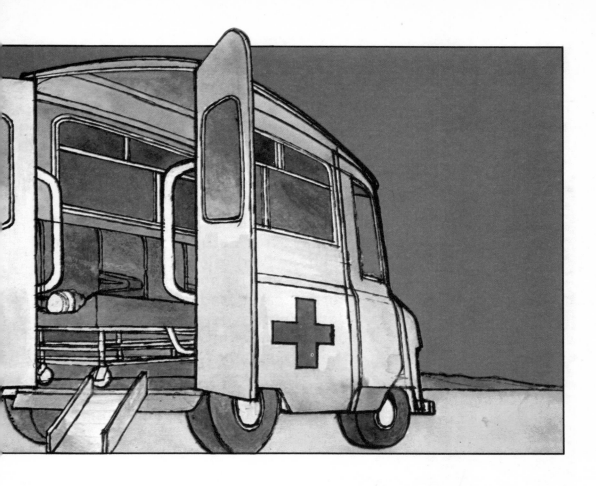

wounded and the prisoners should be cared for and that hospitals and ambulances should not be attacked.

The Society chose a red cross on a white background as their emblem. It is painted on hospital roofs and on ambulances. It is marked on decks of hospital ships and on airfields where planes and helicopters land medical supplies and pick up the wounded. Red Cross nurses and doctors wear the cross on their uniforms.

Red Cross workers also help refugees and people who have lost their homes in fires, earthquakes or floods. They help in hospitals, at football matches and concerts.

Most Red Cross workers are volunteers and receive little or no pay. Young people can join the International Red Cross as cadets. They learn first aid, water safety, and help disabled and elderly people.

Which kinds of rock trap oil?

The Earth has a very hilly surface. It is covered with high mountains and deep valleys. The surface of the Earth has been changing its shape for millions of years. Far below the ground, layers of rock twisted and folded. When they collided, great zigzag creases raised high hills and made deep valleys. Even today, the Earth is still changing its shape very slowly.

Soil and plants on the Earth's surface are gradually pressed down into a hard crust. They become new layers of rock. So the rocks nearest the surface are the newest. The ones that lie deep within the Earth are millions of years old.

The oldest rocks were formed when fiery volcanoes poured out rivers of hot, bubbling lava which cooled into hard rock. Many millions of years later, when dinosaurs lumbered through the forests and swamps, new kinds of rocks formed.

The volcanic rocks were hard and smooth, but the newer ones were sandy and crumbly. They were full of small holes containing drops of water and bubbles of air.

As more layers of rock formed, these spongy rocks were pressed together. The air, water and remains of decayed plants and animals, trapped between the rocks, turned into a thick, dark, sticky mixture. This mixture is oil.

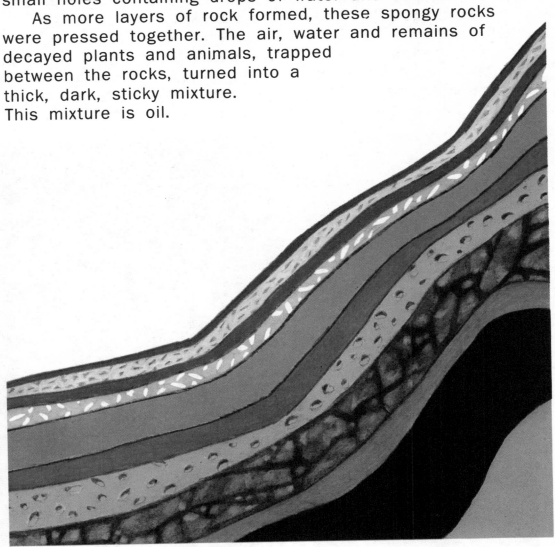

Who shamed the Emperor?

An old Chinese story tells how the Emperor of Peking summoned his cannon-maker. 'Make me a wonderful bell,' he ordered. 'Use all the richest, most valuable metals. Have it ready to ring out over the city in my honour in exactly one year's time.' The cannon-maker did not know how to cast bells, but he had to obey the Emperor.

For twelve months he struggled with the task. Huge urns of red hot brass, silver, gold and iron were poured into the mould. But the metals would not mix and the mould cracked. The Emperor was furious, and ordered that the cannon-maker shoud have his head cut off. Ko-ai, the cannon-maker's daughter, pleaded with the Emperor for her father's life. The Emperor allowed the cannon-maker a further six months.

Again and again, the cannon-maker tried and failed, while the Emperor grew more and more angry. In desperation, Ko-ai travelled the country looking for someone expert in metals who might help. At long last she met a magician who told her what to do: 'Only if you throw yourself into the boiling mixture will the metals mix.'

On the final day, the Emperor arrived at the forge to watch the last attempt to make the bell. But as the frightened cannon-maker poured the hissing, frothing liquid into the mould, Ko-ai leapt in to her death. Immediately the mixture cooled and set. The Emperor was so shocked and ashamed, that he promised that the bell would always ring out in Ko-ai's honour to remind everyone of her bravery.

What is the Sphinx?

On the banks of the Nile near Cairo stands a great stone statue called the Sphinx. It guards the pyramid tomb of King Chephren. Its head is thought to be an image of the Egyptian king himself, but its low, crouching body is that of a lion. No one who saw the stern statue would dare approach or harm the king's grave, for this creature was worshipped as a god.

Other sphinxes guarded many tombs of royal Egyptian kings and queens. Sometimes they had the wings and head of a hawk, or the head of a ram.

What is a man-eater?

For almost a year, two man-eating lions terrorized gangs of workers, who were building a railway line across East Africa. The man-eaters crept into the workmen's camps at night, pulled their victims into tents, and dragged them off into the bush to eat. Even thick fences of thorny spikes set around the camps did not keep the lions out.

A hunter called Colonel Patterson tracked the lions for months, set traps for them and tried to protect the workmen. He had several narrow escapes himself.

One night he lured the man-eaters into an ambush using the carcass of a goat, but it took many bullets to kill each beast.

Who played with the first toys?

If you could join a group of children playing in a street in Ancient Greece, you would probably recognize all their toys, although they might be made and used differently. One child might be skipping with a rope and another bowling or jumping through a hoop. The hoop would be made of heavy bronze. Greek children enjoyed plenty of physical exercise, for strength and fitness were important to the Ancient Greeks.

A group of children might be crouching over a game of marbles. Their marbles would be made of stone or clay and possibly as much as six centimetres wide. Other children might be tossing knucklebones like today's game of jacks. The Greeks enjoyed games where skill and accuracy were involved. Spinning tops made of carved wood or stone and decorated in painted patterns were also popular toys.

In 1922, archaeologists discovered an untouched tomb in the Valley of Kings in Egypt. It belonged to the boy king Tutankhamun who ruled three thousand years ago. Around his preserved corpse, or mummy, lay a boat and a game of draughts to entertain his spirit. Children who lived then played with toys like this carved cat, a horse on wheels, a spoon doll, a jackal's head and cloth balls covered with reeds.

Even before the time of Tutankhamun, children in China and other Eastern countries played with toys we would recognize today: tops to spin, rattles to amuse babies, and moveable wooden and clay dolls. Kites and yo-yos were two of the earliest Chinese toys.

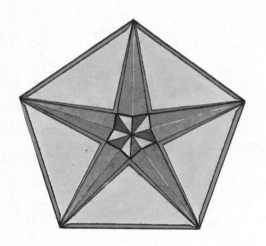

Which signs and numbers are considered to be lucky?

The pentangle is a magic sign. It was used in the Middle Ages by astrologers who studied the mysteries of the stars and planets. It was marked over doorways as a charm to keep away witches and evil spirits.

The pentangle is made up of five straight lines formed into a five-pointed star. Try to draw it without taking your pencil off the paper.

Here is a magical alphabet. The signs are said to have special magical powers. Write your name using the signs instead of letters.

A	B	C	D	E	F	G	H	I

J	K	L	M	N	O	P	Q	R

S	T	U	V	W	X	Y	Z

10

72

3 is a very lucky number as it is considered both magical and holy. There are many stories about three heroes who were triplets. In the Bible three angels guard the throne of God. In the East, the third day of the new moon is the luckiest.

4 is the luckiest of the even numbers. It represents the elements: air, earth, fire and water. Finding a four-leafed clover is said to bring you luck.

7 is an especially lucky number in reading tea leaves. It is also a magical number which often appears in fairy tales. The seventh child of the seventh child is said to have special powers to foretell the future.

13 is an unlucky number. The twelve gods of Norse mythology were feasting when the mischievous Loki joined them. He started a quarrel and one of the gods was killed. Perhaps for this reason it is considered bad luck to sit thirteen people at table. You can calculate your own lucky number. Write down the day, month and year of your birth in numbers (as 16 + 5 + 1969) and add them up (37). Keep adding the digits together until you get a one figure number (3 + 7 = 10; 1 + 0 = 1). That is your lucky birth number.

What is sunken treasure?

Sunken treasure lies scattered over the seabed in many parts of the world. Modern metal detectors and diving equipment make it easier to recover, but is the treasure really worth looking for in the first place?

In 1737 a large ship called the Wendela set sail from the port of Copenhagen in Denmark. The ship was carrying gold coins and bars of silver which were to be traded for silks, tea, spices and perfumes in India. As the ship rounded the Shetland Islands north of Scotland, a great gale blew up. Strong winds and waves drove the ship onto the rocks, where it smashed to pieces and sank.

The crew drowned, but bits of wreckage from the ship washed ashore. Islanders set off with hooks and nets to see what they could rescue. Treasure hunters dived down to search underwater, but the pickings were poor. Most of the treasure was not recovered.

Recently a team of divers set out to search for the rest of the Wendela's treasure. Because of their modern diving equipment the divers could stay underwater for hours at a time and hunt among the nooks and crannies of the seabed. Finally the divers found the rotten shipwreck, which was encrusted with shells and slimy with seaweed. Bags of old silver coins from Holland and Denmark and gold coins from Spain lay spread around the wreck. The divers also found cannons, the ship's anchor and heavy metal bullets.

Who wore red uniforms?

In 1415 English soldiers crossing to France wore red scarves over their coats. This was one of the first pieces of red uniform to be worn by soldiers in Europe.

Henry VII of England later dressed his guards all in red. In the seventeenth century Oliver Cromwell adopted the red uniform for every soldier in his new Model Army. From then on several European kings clothed their armies in fine, scarlet uniforms with magnificent gold braid and lace trimmings.

British soldiers were once nicknamed Red Coats because of their bright red uniforms. Two hundred years ago, during the War of American Independence, they looked a magnificent sight in these fine uniforms, but their bright red jackets made them easy targets for their enemy.

By the end of the nineteenth century, uniforms had become so decorative that they made it hard for soldiers to move quickly or approach their enemy unseen. So uniforms had to become more practical. They were made out of lighter, tougher material, in a dull shade of brown called khaki. This gave better camouflage to the soldiers.

Today red uniforms are ornamental and are worn by special guards and soldiers on grand occasions. The Yeomen of the Guard, who look after the Tower of London, wear the same antique uniform today as when they were established by Henry VII in the fifteenth century. They are often called Beefeaters.

The Royal Canadian Mounted Police Force was formed in the nineteenth century to keep law and order. They became known for their great courage and bravery. Today, the Mounties are a modern police force. On special occasions they still parade wearing their superb uniforms.

How do you tell the time at sea?

On board ship, sailors tell the time by bells. The ship's bell sounds every half hour, ringing one stroke, then two, and so on until eight strokes sound. Half an hour later, this pattern starts again with a single stroke. Time at sea is measured in a different way from on land. The day is divided into six periods called watches. Each watch lasts four hours. The first watch starts at midday.

Sometimes the ship passes a bell buoy which warns of rocks or sand banks just below the surface. The bell sounds as the buoy bobs on the waves. Sometimes a special microphone in the hold of the ship picks up underwater signals. Submarine bells may be fixed to the sunken base of lighthouses to warn of shallow seas.

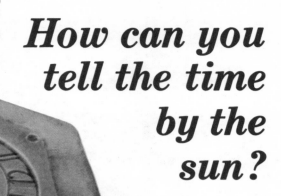

How can you tell the time by the sun?

Long before clocks were invented, people told the time by watching the position of the sun in the sky. They knew that when the sun was low in the east, it must be early morning, when the sun was overhead, it was midday, and when it sank below the horizon in the west, it was evening.

This was not a very accurate way of time-telling. It was difficult to tell whether it was half past eleven or a quarter to twelve just from the position of the sun.

Mathematicians in ancient times invented a shadow clock called a sundial. They marked a circle with the hours of the day from sunrise to sunset. A thin stick was pegged in the centre of the circle. As the sun passed overhead, the stick threw a shadow across the face of the dial, pointing directly to the correct hour of the day.

What is falconry?

The sport of hawking, or falconry, started in Asia about five thousand years ago. One rich Middle Eastern prince kept over seven thousand hawks in his mews, the building where hawks are kept. Marco Polo reported that Genghis Khan had over ten thousand falconers training his birds. In Asia, eagles were sometimes used to hunt wolves, foxes and antelopes.

A nobleman would often hunt on horseback with the falcon perched on his wrist. His arm was protected by a thick leather glove called a gauntlet. When the game was sighted, the falcon was unhooded and released so that it could attack. Seizing its prey, the bird dropped to the ground awaiting its master. Falcons and hawks were mainly used to hunt pheasant, grouse and rabbits.

Falconry remained a favourite sport until the seventeenth century when the use of guns became common. It is still enjoyed among the wealthy Arab sheikhs in the Middle East. Elsewhere falconry is practised only by people who love training falcons. Today falcons are used to clear airfields of smaller birds which may cause accidents.

Falcons and hawks can be taught to hunt smaller birds and animals for their owners. But training a falcon takes enormous patience and time. When the birds are young, they are taught to perch on a thick leather glove at the end of the falconer's outstretched arm. He slips a hood over the bird's head to keep it quiet and fastens its feet with a leather strap. The bird is carefully taught to accept small chunks of meat from the falconer's hand. It slowly gets used to his voice and to being carried around out of doors.

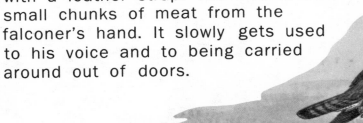

Later, the bird is released on short flights and trained to return to its master's arm. It practises chasing and catching moving prey with a lure, a chunk of meat tied to a long rope. The lure is swung through the air, and the bird is encouraged to attack the meat and return it to the falconer. Eventually, the bird learns to hunt small birds and return them to its master. A good falcon will succeed in killing two out of three times.

Who played with wax dolls?

The first baby dolls were made nearly two hundred years ago. Most were modelled in wax with round chubby faces and bodies.

Some dolls had moving eyes, which opened and closed when a wire was pulled at the back of the body. The doll's hair was usually real human hair. Each strand was stuck into the head while the wax was still soft.

The bodies were usually made of fabric stuffed firm with sawdust or bran. There were also fragile china dolls. Rubber dolls appeared around 1850. They were popular because they could not break. Today, modern plastics are used to make very lifelike dolls.

When dolls' houses first appeared they were called dolls' cabinets. They were often built as playthings for adults and were designed more as museum pieces than toys.

In 1924, a famous English architect designed and built a beautiful doll's house as a gift for Queen Mary. Although fifty-seven years old, the Queen was thrilled with the idea. She took a great interest in all the details of furnishing and decoration. The tiny rooms were lit by fine crystal chandeliers and running water flowed from the kitchen and bathroom taps. Famous painters and furniture makers made miniature copies of their most famous works. Even the books in the library were written by the authors themselves in tiny handwriting.

Why do volcanoes erupt?

When the Earth was first formed, it was very hot. As the Earth cooled, its surface was covered in liquid. Gradually as the Earth grew even cooler, this liquid became the layers of rock that make up the Earth's crust today. Our mountains were made from layers of rock that piled up, and our valleys are the hollows left by the sliding rocks.

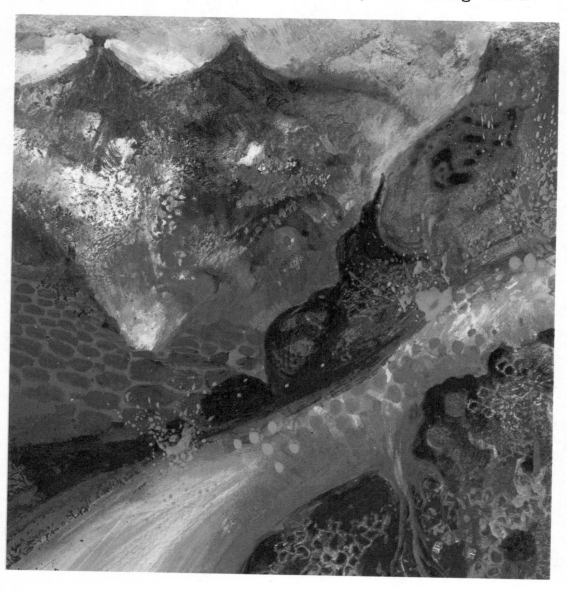

Even today, far below the Earth's cool hard crust, the heat is so great that rocks there are melted or molten. Molten rocks are called magma. Air is trapped between molten rocks. It is squeezed until it forms a powerful gas. The magma and the gas find a weak place in the Earth's crust where the rocks are split and cracked. Then the magma and gas burst violently upwards, melting an escape route for themselves as they go.

At the surface of the Earth, the gas blasts out of the vent, carrying with it lumps of magma, dust and ash.

Sometimes the magma spills out and flows down the mountainside in a molten stream. As it flows it cools to form grey rocks called lava.

Which animals wear bells?

In remote parts of the world, where animals might easily get lost among craggy mountains or in deep forests, bells are tied to them.

In Switzerland, beautifully carved and painted bells are hung around the necks of cows as they graze. Some herders believe this gentle sound keeps the cows contented.

Falcons often hunt with two tiny bells attached to their legs in case they fail to return to their hunter with the prey.

Desert sandstorms continually change the shapes of the dunes and valleys, so it is easy for resting camels to be buried. The faint tinkle of their neck bells guides their owners to them.

After a day's work hauling logs in the Indian forests, the elephants rejoin the herd for the night. They wear wooden bells that make a hollow musical note. Each owner can detect the bell of his own animal.

Who says you're not superstitious?

Even today, when scientists can explain many things that happen in the world, some people still believe in the power of magic. Our ancestors thought they could control spirits with charms and spells. Some of these have been passed down from generation to generation and have become part of our way of life. Children still sometimes chant this old rhyme, when they see an ambulance pass, to protect themselves from accidents.

Touch collar,
Never swallow,
Never get fever,

Touch your nose,
Touch your toes,
Never get on one of those.

Many old beliefs or superstitions make us behave in certain ways. People walk around a ladder rather than underneath it. There may be some sense in this, but why should it be unlucky to open an umbrella indoors?

Some people throw spilt salt over their left shoulders, wear patched clothes or catch falling leaves to bring them good luck. Others may wear sprigs of white heather in their buttonholes, carry stones with holes in them, or wear locks of hair around their necks.

Old shoes to kick at evil spirits are tied behind the car of a newly-married couple when they leave on their honeymoon. Friends throw confetti over them in hope that the couple will have many children.

What is camouflage?

One of the most beautiful owls is the Snowy Owl which lives in the Arctic. Unlike other owls, the Snowy Owl hunts by day. During the Arctic summer, the sun never sets, and in winter, it uses the few short hours of daylight with keenness for food is very scarce. Its main prey, the small mouse-like animal called the lemming, is hibernating. Fish are trapped under the ice and smaller birds have migrated south to warmer climates.

It is for this reason that the feathers of the male bird are almost pure white. They blend, or camouflage, with the snow-covered land and ice around. The female Snowy Owl has small grey-brown flecks in her feathers to camouflage her as she nests on the ground. This helps hide her from wolves and foxes who try to rob her nest.

In different parts of the world, big cats also have coats with different markings which will help them stalk their prey unseen.

The light haired northern lynx hunts in the snow-covered mountains of Canada. It pounces on young deer and rabbits from its perch on a low branch.

The puma is brown and lives among the earth-coloured Rocky Mountains of North America.

The cheetah can run faster than any other land animal. Its spotted fur is like the shadowed undergrowth, so that it can creep up on its victim.

The Bengal tiger lurks in the tall grass of the Indian jungles. Its striped coat blends with the strong shadows of the undergrowth.

The leopard is spotted, as are the ocelot and the jaguar. These animals are hidden by the dappled patterns of the jungle.

How are fires put out?

One method of putting out a fire is to cool the flames. The simplest way is to pour water over them. When we put out a flame, we extinguish it.

One of the best ways to extinguish a dangerous fire is to starve it of oxygen. A girl has accidentally set her skirt alight by going too near the fire. She must be helped before the flames spread. A thick rug is wrapped tightly around her. The air cannot reach the flames burning the skirt. Without air, the fire dies. The girl is saved from being severely burnt.

In large forests there are often lookout towers. The guards on duty watch for a tell-tale wisp of smoke.
When a guard spots a fire, he radios headquarters. A helicopter flies off to find the position of the fire. The pilot reports which way the wind is blowing the fire.
Firemen set off in jeeps and Land Rovers. They move to a position ahead of the fire.
The firefighters clear a wide pathway, called a firebreak, around the fire.

They dig a trench and uproot dry undergrowth so the flames cannot leap across the firebreak and spread any further. In the end, the fire will burn itself out. Sometimes firefighters in fireproof clothing, are parachuted with their equipment into the area of the fire.

Which animals produce dye?

The female cochineal beetle lays her eggs on the large leaves of a cactus which grows in the hot deserts of Central America and Australia. People in Mexico gather the beetles. They crush the dried beetles into a fine powder which they mix with water to make a rich dye. They need about 150,000 beetles to make one kilo of dye.

Cochineal dye was imported to Europe to dye splendid uniforms for soldiers, royal robes and bold flags. Today

Cochineal dye was imported to Europe to dye splendid uniforms for soldiers, royal robes and bold flags. Today artificial dyes are used instead. Cochineal dye is used to colour cake icing, puddings and sweets. Is there a bottle of cochineal or other food colouring in your kitchen? Add a drop to your glass of milk, or dye a boiled egg by adding a few drops of cochineal to the boiling water.

Roman divers searched for the murex shell that lives on rocks beneath the sea. Its body contains a liquid which was used as a deep purple dye. The Roman Emperors and senators wore robes dyed purple from the murex shell.

Why does your heart beat?

Your heart is a pump that drives the blood on its journey around your body. Put your hand on the left side of your rib cage. Can you feel your heart pumping? Every few seconds it pumps your blood through tubes called veins and arteries. A grown person has about five litres of blood, which are pumped around the body about twice a minute.

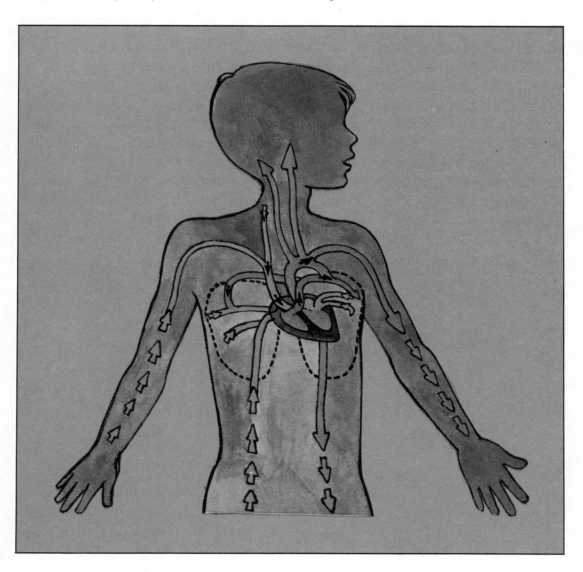

Why does a bull charge red? It doesn't!

An angry bull will charge at anything that moves. It need not be a red rag. Bulls are colour blind and cannot see red or any other colour. But by tradition the cloak of the matador, or bullfighter, is red on one side. This adds to the colour and excitement of the bullfight.

The bull is specially bred to be savage and strong. When the matador waves his red cloak, the bull gets angry. He charges the matador, who sidesteps gracefully to avoid the bull's sharp horns. Finally the matador pierces the bull with his sword.

Although many people believe bullfighting is cruel, in Spain and South America the sport has been admired for centuries as a display of daring and skill.

How did puppet shows begin?

For hundreds of years Punch and Judy shows have been performed in many countries. At seaside resorts and fairs, children cluster around the small red and white striped puppet theatre and laugh with delight at Punch's naughty antics.

Punch probably came into being in Roman times, when actors wore strange masks to act out their plays. Much later on, in France, Punch became the puppet we know today, with his hooked nose, hunchback and squeaky voice. He was first brought to England over three hundred years ago, and other characters were introduced to act in the plays. Today he has a wife called Judy and a baby. There are also a doctor, a police officer, a hangman and a devil.

Punch causes dreadful trouble by knocking the other puppets over the head with his stick. He always avoids punishment and everyone else takes the blame. His dog Toby is his only friend. Toby frightens away the devil with the bells on his neck frill.

The early puppet theatres travelled from town to town entertaining people with ancient legends, the adventures of bold heroes, fables and many of the Bible stories. Many different kinds of puppets were used all over the world.

String puppets or marionettes are wired to a crossbar. The arms, legs, head and body can all be made to move independently and perform very lifelike movements.

A glove puppet fits over the hand. The first and second fingers support the puppet's head, and the two end fingers and thumb work its arms.

A sock puppet is pulled over the arm and the clenched fist forms the head. Finger puppets fit onto each finger and cannot be moved so freely.

Shadow puppets were invented many centuries ago by the ancient Chinese people. The limbs of these flat cut-out figures are attached to sticks. As the puppets move between a strong light and the backcloth, they throw moving shadows in silhouette.

Who had a Chariot of Gold?

Long ago, people believed that the Earth stood still and the sun took a journey across the sky each day.

The ancient Greeks believed that the sun was the god Apollo, travelling through the sky in his chariot of dazzling gold, drawn by eight magnificent horses with golden harnesses.

They thought that each morning Apollo rose from the bottom of the sea in his chariot. During the day he drove in splendour across the sky. As twilight came, he plunged once more into the waves, where a golden ship waited to carry him home again. In the morning, he mounted his chariot and started his journey once more.

Why were pyramids built?

The ancient Egyptians also worshipped the sun. One of the names for their sun god was Ra.

The kings and queens of Egypt were called pharaohs. Each pharaoh was worshipped as a sun god, too, and was called a son of the sun god.

The Egyptians believed that their sun god rode across the sky each day and that when a pharaoh died, he joined his father in the sky. Every pharaoh planned a great tomb in which he would be buried. The tomb rose in a great pyramid.

Each pyramid had four sides. One of the sides faced east. The Egyptians believed that when their pharaoh died, he watched his father's approach as the sun rose in the east. At midday the sun's rays fell down all four slopes. They formed a staircase of light up which the pharaoh's soul climbed.

How are animals threatened?

For centuries, lions have been hunted by people. Lions were driven from the grassy plains that stretched across Europe to Russia, as land was cleared for farmland. In India, the last large group of Asian lions is likely to die out soon, as their safe home in the Gir Forest is threatened and changed by hunters and farmers. Large numbers of lions are now found only in East Africa.

Safari hunters matched their skill and courage against the strength of the lion. They stalked and killed him at close range with powerful guns. Lion skins were sold to make rugs, coats and bags.

Today we realize that many species of wild animal must be protected if they are to survive. Laws have been passed in Africa and India to prevent too many lions being killed. But tribesmen still break the law, setting cruel traps to catch the animals. When such poachers are caught, they are severely punished.

Another major cause of danger to animal and plant life is pollution. This can occur both on land and at sea. As life on land becomes more and more crowded, it is becoming increasingly important that we control pollution with strict laws. We should take care not to destroy the oceans in the same way as we have carelessly ruined large areas of land.

There are strict laws to prevent oil spills, but accidents do happen. Slicks of oil collect on the waves and the tide carries them ashore. They kill plants growing on the sea shore and fish in the water. The feathers of sea birds get clogged and matted, so they cannot fly. They peck at the oil to clean their feathers, and it poisons them. Hundreds of dead fish and birds are washed up on the beaches after a large oil slick.

Who works on an oil rig?

The oil rig is like a small island far out at sea. Strong gales lash the steel girders. High waves break fiercely against the legs. Sometimes a sea mist creeps in and cuts off the rig from the supply ships which bring food and equipment.

The cranes and drilling equipment are on top of the platform of the oil rig. The crew's quarters are below deck. The rig hums with activity day and night. Work goes on twenty-four hours a day in shifts.

In their sleeping quarters, the workmen, who are off-duty, play cards, read books or watch films. Their work is exhausting. After a few weeks on the rig, they fly home by helicopter for a week's holiday.

Everybody on the oil rig is part of a team and has an important job to do. There may be as many as sixty men working on the oil rig at a time. The drill superintendent is in charge of the rig. He organizes the drilling programme with the help of geologists, scientists, weathermen and engineers. He gives orders to the foremen, who are known as toolpushers. They, in turn, organize the gangs of workmen. The workmen are known as roustabouts.

The divers make daily underwater checks to the rig. They clean the rust from the girders and scrape barnacles off the pontoons and legs.

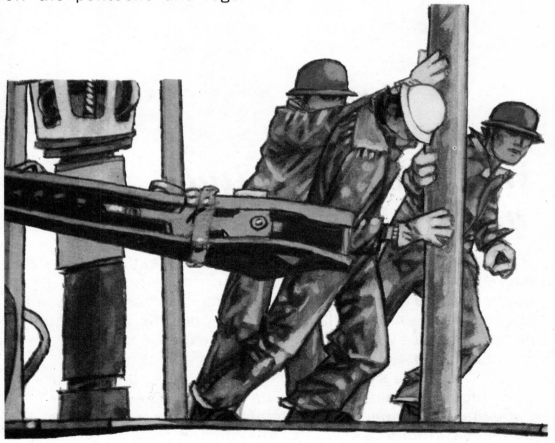

Where can you find magical toys?

The ballet *Coppélia* tells the story of a beautiful life-size puppet which has been modelled by the strange old Dr Coppelius. He hopes to make the puppet come alive with magic spells and by filling her with the life of a human being. He lures a young village lad called Franz into his workshop and puts him to sleep with a potion.

Dr Coppelius's evil magic is upset by a girl called Swanhilda who has been spying on him. Dressed in Coppelia's clothing, she pretends to come alive as Dr Coppelius chants his spells. The doctor thinks his magic

has worked as Swanhilda dances around the room. But her dance grows so wild that she destroys everything in the workshop and then escapes with Franz.

The world's most famous ballet about toys is *The Nutcracker*. Clara is given a wonderful carved nutcracker as a Christmas present. At midnight she creeps downstairs and sees the nutcracker leading a battalion of toy soldiers into battle against the terrifying mouse king and his army. Just as the mouse king is about to attack the nutcracker, Clara throws her slipper and kills the mouse king. This breaks the enchantment and the nutcracker turns into a handsome prince and takes Clara off to the Land of Sweets. In the morning Clara awakes to discover it all was a dream.

What makes red and infra-red?

Light from the sun travels to the earth in waves. These waves are tiny and move very fast.

Although sunlight looks white to us, it is made up of seven different colours. These colours move so quickly that they mix together and appear as 'white light'. The colours that make up light are the colours of the rainbow: red, orange, yellow, green, blue, indigo and violet. This band of colours is called the spectrum.

When light shines on an object, we can see it. Without light, the object is dark and hidden. Some of the light which shines on the object reflects and bounces off again.

A coloured object takes in, or absorbs, all the colours except its own. A red flag absorbs all the colours in the spectrum except red. It reflects red, which is why it looks red to us.

The sun gives off heat as well as light. The heat travels to earth in waves, which warm the ground and help plants and animals to grow.

When a candle or light bulb burns, it gives off heat. The heat spreads, or radiates, just like the heat from the sun.

These heat waves are invisible and are known as infra-red. They are called infra-red because they are beyond red in the spectrum. They are longer than ordinary red light waves

We use infra-red light in many ways. Infra-red ovens in car factories dry the paint on cars rapidly. Smaller infra-red ovens are used in restaurants to cook food very quickly. Special cameras using infra-red film can take pictures in the dark.

Why do hawks have good eyesight?

People with good eyesight are said to have eyes like a hawk because hunting birds have very sharp eyesight. Their eyes are set forward high above their beaks. Both eyes can scan the same area and pinpoint moving objects very accurately. Each eye also has good side vision, so the bird does not need to move its head from left to right. The bird's eyes are hooded by a strong arch of bone which protects them.

Birds of prey look glaring and fierce because of the way their eyes stare and gleam. Like all birds, they have a third eyelid which is transparent. Each time the bird blinks, the lid passes over the eye to clean and moisten the eyeball. It also shields the eye from strong sunlight or attack.

Why do birds of prey store their food?

Birds of prey eat small birds, fish, reptiles, large insects and small mammals. They only eat when they are hungry. After a big meal, they may not eat for several days, or even weeks. Having made its kill, a bird of prey usually carries the food back to the nest before eating it.
But sometimes the arrival of other thieving birds forces it to gobble down its meal in a hurry. It swallows great chunks of fur, flesh and bone.

The unchewed food is stored in a special stomach called a gizzard. Flesh and smaller bones slowly dissolve there, but fur and larger bones are coughed up several hours later in a small clump called a pellet. Pellets are often found near the nest of a bird of prey. By examining them, you can tell what the bird has eaten.

What is your fortune?

The gypsy fortune-teller gazes deeply into a crystal ball in front of her. She seems to see moving pictures, shapes and words hidden in the glass. Slowly, she explains their mysterious meanings. She recalls things that happened long ago to her customer, and foretells events to come.

The palms of your hands are criss-crossed with lines and the gypsy fortune-teller may try to predict your future by looking at them. Everbody has different patterns on their palms and fingers but very few hands have all the lines shown. If you are right-handed the palmist reads your right hand to see what you will make of your life, while your left hand shows the possibilities with which you were born. If you are left-handed it is exactly the reverse. Palmistry is a very ancient art which was practised in the Far East at least five thousand years ago.

All cards can be used for fortune-telling, but sometimes a special pack called the Tarot is used. Tarot cards are supposed to be especially magical and their origin is ancient and mysterious.

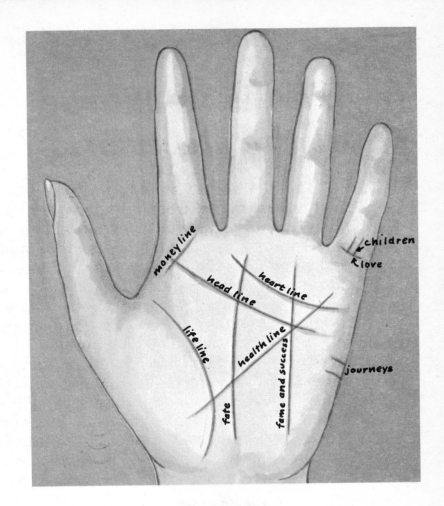

There are many ways of using a Tarot pack. One of them is to tell the future by using the Clock, or Circle, spread method. 12 cards are laid down in a circle and a 13th is placed in the middle. Card 13 is read first as a forecast for the whole year; then the others are read one by one. If the cards are laid upside down their meanings change.

Who is in charge at the steelworks?

At the steelworks, shining steel tubes, bars and smooth sheets are made from rocks of iron ore. It is a hot and noisy place. Huge furnaces are filled with iron ore and coke and as the metal heats and melts, it glows orange and yellow, and finally pours out into a mould in a running stream of white-hot liquid.

In the mould, the iron cools into a rough shaped bar. It must now be rolled, pressed and shaped by great machines controlled by computers. The computer has been given a programme which lets it know what size the bar should be. The computer decides how fast the bar should pass between the giant rollers, and how firmly they should squeeze it. It sends signals to the machines to make them press harder or roll faster so that the steel bar will come out the right shape.

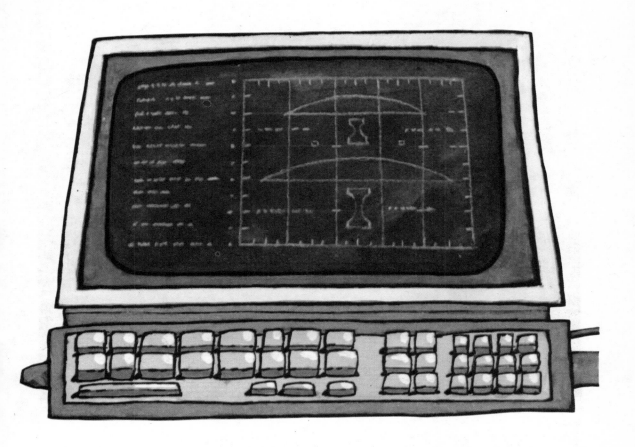

The same computer can do other jobs at the steelworks. Just as you can make a model to show you how a ship or a plane works, the computer can make a model of a steel bridge or steel crane. It doesn't actually make a small model, but it can make detailed plans, showing exactly what steel bars will be needed, how long and how tough they must be, and where they will need to take plenty of strain. It may show its plans on a screen to help the scientists and engineers at the factory.

As well as helping with steel making, the computer may also be used to calculate the wages of the steelworkers. It also keeps a check of all the stocks of metal and makes sure that there is enough steel being made to supply all the customers.

What was the Legend of Popocatepetl?

Two high peaks tower above the other mountains of Mexico. The mountain, Ixtaccihuatl, is covered with snow and is very beautiful. The other is a snow-capped volcano, Popocatepetl. It is not an explosive volcano, but it does pour out a continuous cloud of smoke.

The Mexicans tell a story about their smoking mountain. They believe that Ixtaccihuatl was a beautiful princess, daughter of a powerful Mexican king who had many enemies. The king promised that his daughter would marry the man who defeated his enemies. Popocatepetl loved the princess and he set off to fight for her hand.

Popocatepetl finally defeated all the king's enemies and started triumphantly for home to claim his bride. But before he reached the palace, jealous enemies sent false news of his death to the princess. She was so upset that she became ill and died.

When Popocatepetl arrived home and discovered that she was dead, he too wanted to die. He built two great pyramids next to each other. He laid the body of Ixtaccihuatl on top of one pyramid and he stood on top of the other, lighting her tomb with a flaming torch.

As the years passed, snow covered the pyramids and the lovers, but the torch continues to smoke to this day.

Which animal is the King of the beasts?

The colours of the African bush are the sandy, gold and brown colours of dry grass and thorn trees. The lion's coat is the same tawny shade, and so he moves unseen, camouflaged against the background.

There are small tufts of hair on the lion's elbows and behind his ears. Another tassel of hair hides the tiny claw on the tip of his tail. The hair around his chin and

whiskers is almost white. His head is crowned with a shaggy mane and beard which give him a fierce, proud look. When an enemy approaches, he puffs out his mane to look even more menacing. The lioness does not have this long hair. Like the peacock or the stag, the male of this species appears more splendid than the female.

Who were the pirates?

There have been pirates ever since people traded across the seas. In Greek and Roman times, pirates lurked in creeks and caves around the Mediterranean Sea. They were ready to attack passing boats to steal the goods on board. Heavy wooden galleys, moving slowly through the water, were favourite targets. Even when the galley sails were hoisted, the pirates in their smaller, faster boats could overtake the bigger ships.

Trading ships were crammed with valuable goods. They were owned by merchants, who traded timber for jewels, silks for perfumes, and carpets for silver coins. Each ship was a temptation to pirates.

The goods stolen from a ship are called booty. The captain rewarded his pirate crew with a share of the booty in return for hard work and brave fighting. Of course, the captain kept the largest share for himself from the choice of pearls from the Pacific, silks and perfumes from China, gold statues from Mexico, carpets from Arabia, ivory from Africa, and spices, jewels and cottons from India.

People became pirates for different reasons.

Many of them were wanted men, who had committed crimes and fled to escape punishment. Punishments were harsh even for small crimes. A man might have been hanged for stealing a coat. No wonder he ran away! Sailors became pirates, too. Life in the navy was hard, the work was strenuous, the cabins were uncomfortable and the food was bad. Sailors often quarrelled with their captains and ran away to join a band of easy-going pirates.

Other pirates plundered enemy ships for their ruler or government, and were rewarded for their deeds!

Which volcano blew itself to pieces?

Some volcanoes are really islands in the ocean. They begin in the same way as volcanoes on land. A volcanic island starts from a crack in the ocean bed. With each new eruption, fresh layers of lava raise the slopes of the volcano. The mountain grows higher and higher, until its cone suddenly rises above the waves.

Sailors on passing ships are surprised when they find an uncharted island at sea. They are even more astonished when the tiny island starts to puff smoke and erupt violently.

About one hundred years ago a great explosion thundered and rocked the sea in the East Indies. The noise was heard almost five thousand kilometres away. Clouds of ash darkened the sky and settled on ships at sea and on islands for miles around. The air remained black for two days. A giant tidal wave rushed across the ocean, swamping everything in its path and causing terror and destruction.

When everything was quiet again, the volcanic island of Krakatoa had vanished. Only craggy rocks remained around a deep hole that disappeared far into the Earth.

But volcanoes can reappear. Forty years after the explosion, Krakatoa had rebuilt itself. Since then, it has exploded several times and may erupt again.

Where are fish caught?

From the edge of the seashore, the land continues to slope away underwater making a gently tilted ledge. In some places, this ledge continues to slope out to sea for many kilometres. It is called the Continental Shelf.

The water above the Continental Shelf can be 200 metres deep. Sunlight filters through to the bed of the shelf bringing both light and warmth. Since life in the sea, just as life on land, depends on these conditions, sea creatures and plants thrive.

Most of the large quantities of fish that are caught for our food are trapped by fishing boats. Trawlers are large boats that work in the deeper waters of the Continental Shelf. Their nets are cone shaped and are sometimes thirty metres across at the mouth. The boats drag the nets behind them until filled with fish, then they are heaved onto the deck by a winch or crane. The fish are sorted and stored in huge refrigerators below deck until the trawler returns to port.

Trawlers and other types of fishing boat often carry electrical equipment which picks up the sounds made by the movement of large shoals of fish. This helps fishermen move quickly to the right location. In fact, modern equipment has made fishing so much more efficient, that in some places close to the shore, not enough fish are managing to breed. Fishermen find they must travel further and further out to sea for their catch, and this has led to new kinds of deep sea fish arriving on our plates.

Which were the earliest dolls?

The earliest dolls were not really toys at all but carved models of gods or other religious figures. They were worshipped at festivals and ceremonies and were believed to have wonderful magical powers. Each model was decorated as the figure of the god of sun, wind or rain, the spirit of waterfalls or harvests. Many were handed down from generation to generation as family heirlooms. Sometimes the carved figures were given to the children to play with when the ceremony had ended.

In Japan, two doll festivals are held each year, one for girls and one for boys. They have taken place for more than a thousand years, and probably began as ceremonies to worship the Emperor. The most precious dolls that a child can be given are dressed as the Emperor and Empress of Japan.

Toys made by primitive peoples or peasants who live in the countryside are often formed from plants and vegetables.

The American Indians fold large maize leaves into a simple doll shape and paint on a face. More leaves are arranged gracefully around the doll for clothing and these are decorated with native patterns.

The Mexican peasants plait dolls from straw. A stripped maize husk or a large root can also be shaped into a doll. Fruits and vegetables are carved to make heads with strange and amusing faces.

Wooden pestles and spoons and other kitchen utensils provide ideal shapes to make simple dolls and puppets.

How do magicians do tricks?

The earliest recorded magician was Tchatcha-em-ankh, who performed magic tricks at the court of King Khufu of Egypt in 3766 BC. Since then, magicians all over the world have performed what seems to be magic as entertainment.

In India, men dressed in long robes squat in the market place, charming snakes out of baskets and sending small boys up ropes suspended in the air. Chinese magicians walk on fire or climb ladders made of razor-sharp swords.

Modern magicians use many ancient tricks. Conjuring is a matter of practice and no magical powers are needed. A conjuror must perform his tricks so skilfully that the audience are completely baffled by his movements. Often he tries to distract their attention with jokes and chatter while his fingers are preparing some trick.

The conjuror asks the audience to tie his wrists together using the ends of a long length of string. While this is going on, he hands a bracelet to the audience and asks them to make sure it cannot be opened in any way. When his wrists are tied, he turns his back quickly on the audience, and saying 'Abracadabra', he faces them with the bracelet dangling from the string.

Try this trick for yourself while wearing long sleeves. You will need: A length of string, about 50 cms long, and 2 identical bracelets large enough to slip over your wrists. Slide one bracelet up your arm and hide it under your sleeve. When you turn your back to the audience, slip the bracelet the audience has examined into your pocket and slide the other one down your arm and on to the string.

Who were the Aztecs?

People have always marvelled at the magnificence and power of the sun. Some of them worshipped the sun as a god. Even today, people who live very simple or primitive lives worship the sun, which helps keep them alive. Hundreds of years ago, in Central and South America, the sun was worshipped by tribes of clever and scientific people. Their ancestors had worshipped the sun for thousands of years before them. These people believed that the sun protected them and gave them strength over their enemies.

One of these tribes was called the Aztecs. They worshipped several gods. They built cities with fine temples, which climbed in great steps towards the sky. Inside, the temples were decorated with ornate statues of their gods, studded with precious stones. The Aztecs placed treasures of silver and gold in front of the statues.

Who was 'The Sun King'?

In the town of Versailles in France, there is a splendid palace set in elaborate gardens. The gardens blaze with colourful flowers laid out in decorative patterns. Fountains shoot high jets of water into the air. There are bushes clipped into the shapes of birds and animals.

Over three hundred years ago this was the palace of a great king, Louis XIV. When he lived there, the palace blazed with light and throbbed with music. The rooms were filled with silken curtains, embroidered tapestries, elegantly carved furniture and rare ornaments of silver and gold.

The king himself was just as grand and richly decorated as his palace. He wore rich satins and velvets embroidered with fine jewels. Even the heels of his shoes were studded with diamonds! Because Louis XIV was so dazzling, he was known as *'Le Roi Soleil'*. This is French for 'The Sun King'.

What is a curfew?

Houses built hundreds of years ago were made of wood and straw. In towns, houses were built close together around the market place or the church. When one house caught fire, whole streets of houses were destroyed before water could be brought to put out the flames. In the ninth century, Alfred the Great, the King of England, ordered the church bells to be rung each evening at eight o'clock. On the signal, all household fires were to be put out to prevent fires starting from sparks and dying embers. The signal was called the curfew bell. In the days when high walls protected cities, the curfew bell was rung to announce the closing of the city gates.

Today the curfew bell is seldom sounded, although in some countries curfew hours in the evening are still ordered. Then, in troubled areas, nobody is allowed to walk in the streets or they risk being arrested.

Which bells protect people?

Thousands of years ago, bells were used as a form of protection against evil spirits. People were afraid of the spirits of the dead which they believed still haunted the earth. The oldest bells ever found were unearthed in an Egyptian tomb where they were put to drive away the evil spirits. In Ancient Egypt pregnant women wore necklaces of silver and gold bells to protect their unborn babies.

Some jungle tribes in the Pacific Islands hollow out bamboo stalks or large tree roots into the shapes of bells. They ring them in the jungle villages to guide travellers home, or strike them to send messages from one village to another.

Today we use bells on all kinds of occasions to attract people's attention. The first bicycles, like the tall rather wobbly penny farthing, were thought to be so dangerous that a bell jangled from the handlebars.

Why did American Indians worship eagles?

American Indians worshipped the eagle because they believed it healed the sick and brought peace to fighting tribes. Young warriors decorated their headdresses with twelve tail feathers from the Golden Eagle to give them strength and hunting skill. For special ceremonies young girls wore a single feather in their hair. In the south-western United States, the Pueblo Indians dressed up in eagle wings and headdresses to perform beautiful soaring and hunting dances in honour of the eagle.

Some tribes believed that the eagle was sacred. It was forbidden to kill one to get its feathers. The feathers could only be plucked from a living bird. A pit was dug and an Indian warrior crouched in the bottom of it, holding a chunk of meat as a lure. As the bird swooped, he seized its legs and tied them up. The eagle was kept in the Indian camp to provide a constant supply of feathers.

Who made undersea exploration possible?

People dived for shells and shellfish long before any special underwater breathing equipment was designed. Because divers had to hold their breath, they could not stay underwater for very long.

The Ancient Greeks liked to eat oysters. Divers, armed with sharp knives and nets, gathered them from the seabed. Sometimes, the oysters contained beautiful pearls which were made into jewellery. The pearly linings of the insides of the shells were also carved into rich ornaments.

A diver can hold his breath underwater for about three minutes. To stay underwater longer than this, the diver will need some kind of breathing equipment. Many different ideas have been tried.

The Ancient Greeks lowered divers into the sea in an upturned barrel. The divers breathed the air trapped in the barrel. But they soon used up all the oxygen in the air, and they had to rise to the surface quickly.

About two hundred years ago this basic idea was developed into the diving bell. The diving bell, containing the diver, was lowered from a ship into the water. Tubes bringing oxygen from the surface allowed the diver to breathe underwater for about an hour.

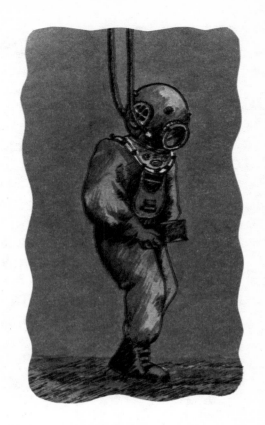

Augustus Siebe invented the first airtight diving suit in 1837. The diver wore a diving suit with a large helmet. Air tubes were attached to the helmet, bringing fresh air from the surface of the sea.

Jacques Cousteau is one of the world's most famous undersea explorers. In 1943 he invented a simple breathing machine called an aqualung or scuba. The diver carries his air supply strapped on his back in cylinders called tanks. A tube carries the air from the tank to the diver's watertight mask. The air flow is controlled by a regulator which supplies air when the diver breathes in. It also makes sure that the pressure of the air is correct for the pressure of the water surrounding the diver. Because the aqualung is light and practical, it allows the diver to swim about freely.

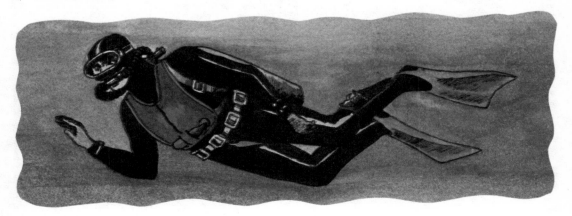

Which beasts are magical?

The griffin is a legendary beast that has the body of a lion, the wings and head of an eagle and the ears of a horse. It has a red front, a blue neck, white wings and black feathers on its back. It is as strong as two hundred eagles and can carry off two oxen in one mighty claw.

Griffins were said to live in the mountains of Scythia, an ancient country near Persia. They spun great nests of gold and fiercely guarded the entrances to hoards of hidden treasure. A group of one-eyed people lived nearby, who liked to plait gold thread into their hair. Sometimes they tried to creep up unseen to steal gold from the griffins' nests. If the griffins caught the thieves, they tore them to pieces before they could escape.

An ancient Egyptian legend tells of a wonderful bird, like a golden eagle, called a Phoenix. At the end of its life, it burned itself to death in a huge fire. Then the Phoenix rose from its own ashes to begin a new life.

When the huge, fossilized bones of dinosaurs were first unearthed, many people believed that these were the remains of dragons. However, dragons are imaginary creatures. They were first mentioned in stories told long ago when they were described as magical lizards. In later tales they became fierce monsters with huge wings, sharp claws, scaly bodies and nostrils that belched fire and smoke.

Where can you visit a volcano?

Mount Etna, on the island of Sicily in the Mediterranean, is an active volcano that erupts every few years. When it erupts, the lava flows down the mountainside. The small villages on the slopes are destroyed. Families lose their homes and possessions.

When the volcano becomes peaceful once again, the slopes are crowded with curious visitors and reporters.

Mount Etna is a magnificent sight. It towers above the rest of the island and pours hot steam and smoke into the air. The warm air rising from the crater soon cools as it meets the colder air above. Thick white clouds form, often hiding the summit from view.

There is a road that winds and twists up Mount Etna as the slope grows steeper. When the volcano is quiet, visitors leave their cars and crowd into cable cars that swing them slowly upwards through the clouds around the summit. At the top, jeeps carry the tourists several miles across the dark, grey wastes of lava and ash towards the crater. No birds fly here; no plants grow, except for a few struggling lichens and patches of green fungus. It is dead and still. The visitors see the choking smoke and fumes. They hear the rumble and hiss of escaping steam. They gaze into the vent that leads into the fiery depths of the Earth.

How are bells made?

Bells are made in a foundry using methods that have not changed much for thousands of years. Foundries were once kept busy making cannons and large weapons, as well as bells. Today, there are only a few foundries left.

The bell founder first makes a clay, sand and mud model of the bell, called a core. Ensuring this is completely dry, he smooths the outside to a shiny gloss with a coating of china clay. He then makes an exact copy of the bell, called a dummy. He models this in clay and wood, pressing it tightly over the core. When dry, a third outer layer, called a cope, is packed over the dummy.

To make a metal bell, copper and tin are mixed together in special proportions, and heated to a very high temperature until red hot and liquid, or molten.

The molten metal is poured through funnels into the mould between the core and the cope. When the metal is cooled, the cope is chipped off, the bell lifted from the core, then cleaned and polished. Much of the skill in bell-making is in the final shaping and tuning. When the bell is beaten by a clapper, the strike note must ring out pure and clear.

The three layers are then separated. The dummy is thrown away, as only the inner core and outer cope are needed. The gap left between them forms the mould for the bell.

The bell is tuned on a lathe. As it spins round, a machine gently files away fine layers of metal from the inside, until the tuner hears that the bell produces pure notes.

Many bells are inscribed with the name of the foundry and date they were cast. They sometimes carry a verse, a quotation or some dedication.

Who was the Red Baron?

Baron Manfred von Richthofen had only one close friend, his Danish hound called Moritz. To everyone else he was cool and distant. His whole life was dedicated to his work — shooting down enemy planes.

Von Richthofen was a German fighter pilot during the First World War. He commanded a unit of fifty-six planes, which became known as the Richthofen Circus. The planes were painted with broad red crosses. His daring command of the Circus and his unbeaten record of destroying enemy planes earned him the nickname of the Red Baron.

Fighter planes in those days were ricketty contraptions, compared with modern jet fighters. The pilot sat alone in an open cockpit. He controlled the plane and fired a machine-gun at the same time.

The Red Baron surprised an enemy plane by swooping down on it out of the clouds. The two aircraft twisted and circled in the sky, trying to avoid each other's bullets. They stalked each other behind thick clouds and looped in great circles. Then they passed very close, shooting at each other's petrol tanks. The Red Baron often followed the blazing enemy plane to the ground to claim a trophy for his collection of pieces of wreckage.

The Red Baron destroyed a record number of eighty enemy planes before he was shot down by a Canadian pilot. He was Germany's greatest ace pilot.

How does a lion spend its day?

The lion wakes lazily. Throughout the hot day he has rested in the shade, saving his energy for hunting. Now it is evening, and he is hungry. As he stretches and arches his backbone, five hundred powerful muscles tighten. Now that he is fully grown, his body is nearly three metres long from his head to the tip of his tail. It is sleek and streamlined.

When he yawns, he bares four pointed fangs and rows of sharp, strong teeth to cut, rip and tear raw meat. His tongue is long and rough like sandpaper. It can strip a bone clean.

The lion gets up on four broad and shaggy paws. Fleshy pads on his heels and under his toes help him to jump and to land with a bouncy spring. When he attacks, his sharp claws dart out.

The lion must eat a lot of meat to keep up his strength so he can protect the pride. Each fortnight he will get through a whole animal. There is little shortage of food, for the grazing herds of gazelle and antelope breed and grow quickly. Without some form of control, their numbers would grow and grow, and soon strip the grassland bare, causing widespread famine. In their own way, the lions help to preserve the balance of wild life in the African bush.

The lioness is the chief hunter. The lion's main duty is to protect the pride from attack. A lioness hunting alone will attack zebra, wildebeeste or gazelle. All these animals are strong runners, and the lioness would tire first in a chase. For this reason, she must rely on a surprise attack. A pride of lions will hunt down bigger game than a lion or lioness on its own. Using an ambush, the pride will attack buffalo or giraffe.

What can you play with on Sundays?

In winter, the great forests of Germany lay deep in snow or crisp with frost and ice. The foresters stayed at home, warming themselves by huge log fires. They told stories and gossiped, while they whittled and carved small toys of wood. They made animals and birds, dolls, carts, wagons and sledges. They painted them in gay colours and gave them to the children as playthings

The German wood carvers grew famous for their toys. At Oberammergau in southern Germany, the carvers formed a union called a guild. They agreed to make toys to a high standard and to sell them cheaply to all parts of the world.

The Oberammergau craftsmen were used to carving religious figures and church furniture. They made beautiful model cribs for Christmas, with the kings, shepherds and angels grouped in the stable at Bethlehem. From Oberammergau came the first Noah's Ark and many of the early dolls' houses.

Until quite recently Sunday was considered to be a day of worship when the strictest rules of behaviour had to be obeyed by all the family. Children were not allowed to play with toys on Sunday, read anything except religious books, nor run and skip about outside in their Sunday clothes.

The only plaything allowed was a Noah's Ark. It was hoped that children would learn the Bible story as they played. There were tiny animals, a male and female of each species, carved in wood and painted. The Ark itself was often very elaborate with separate stables and cages for all the different animals. Hinged doors and windows opened out onto the deck. Noah and his family were standing figures, brightly dressed in peasant costumes.

Why does night fall?

The sun is really a shining star. Although it is about 150 million kilometres away, it is still closer to the Earth than any other star. The sun is near enough to light up the whole sky around us. When the sun's light shines onto our part of the Earth, we do not need candles or electric lights to help us see. There are millions of other stars in the sky. Some are much larger than the sun. But they are all so very, very far away from us that we only see them as tiny pinpoints of light twinkling in the distance.

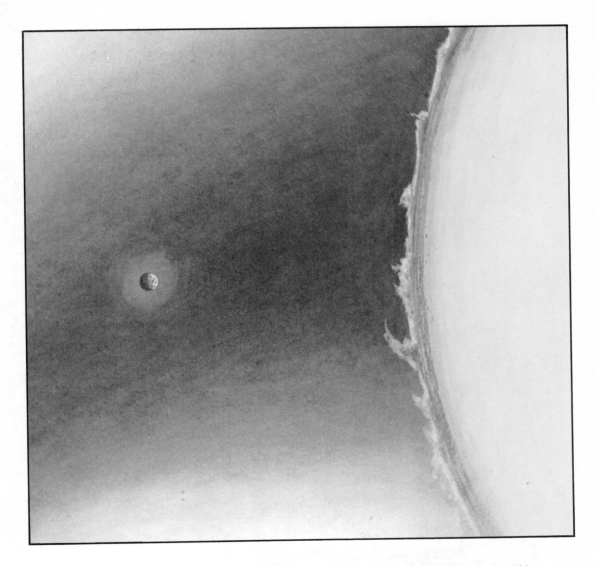

Although it seems flat, the sun is actually round. We know that the Earth is round like a ball, too. Both balls spin around and around in space.

The sun takes nearly one month to spin around once. It always looks the same to us whichever way it is facing. The Earth takes one day and one night to spin around once.

The Earth has no light of its own. It is lit up completely by the sun. On the half of the earth which faces the sun, it is day. On the dark half of the Earth, it is night.

Who was Houdini?

Harry Houdini was a famous American conjuror. His success began when he discovered that very few people can tie a really tight knot, and that handcuffs spring open when they are banged against a wall in a certain way. He trained hard to become fit and strong, and practised breath and muscle control. Ropes that held him firmly when his chest was puffed up and his muscles were tight, slipped off easily when he relaxed his body.

For three hours, Houdini kept his audience spellbound. He challenged them to lock him in chains and handcuffs, tie him in a sack, and padlock him into a trunk, which was then lowered into a tank of water.

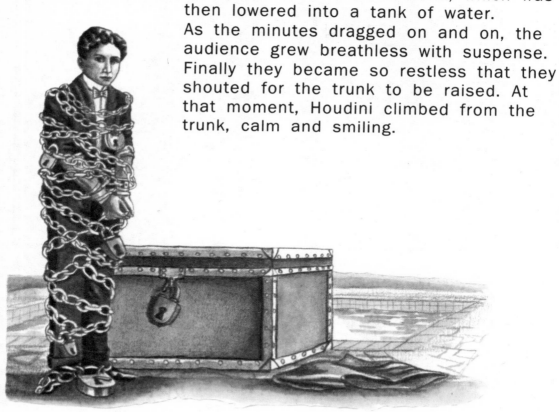

As the minutes dragged on and on, the audience grew breathless with suspense. Finally they became so restless that they shouted for the trunk to be raised. At that moment, Houdini climbed from the trunk, calm and smiling.

Who is Big Ben?

One of the most famous bells in the world is Big Ben. This bell rings the hour chimes in the clock tower of the Houses of Parliament in London. The clock is known as Big Ben too, but the name really belongs to the bell. Some people believe Big Ben may have been named after Sir Benjamin Hall, a large, portly gentleman who supervised the hanging of the bell about one hundred and twenty years ago. Most think it was named after a powerful boxer called Big Ben who won many famous fights in the ring.

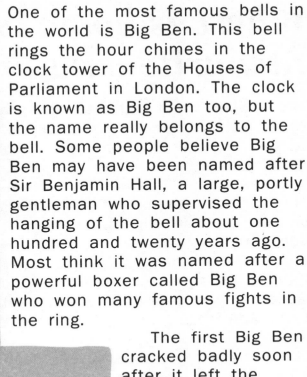

The first Big Ben cracked badly soon after it left the foundry. It was melted down and recast. With great difficulty, it was hauled one hundred metres up the tower. The present Big Ben is also cracked, but because it would be so difficult to lower and recast it will probably never be mended. The clapper strikes the bell on the part which is not cracked, so the chimes ring out loud and clear.

Where is home to many favourite wild animals?

The African bush, with its rich grassland and scattered water holes, provides an ideal home for many animals. Some, like the antelope, are herbivorous; they eat grass, grazing together in large herds.

Others, like the lion, are meat-eating or carnivorous. They prey on grazing herds for their food. Hyenas and jackals are scavengers. They wait for the remains of the lion's meal.

The elephant is the largest animal that lives on land. It uses its trunk like a giant hand to scoop up grass and thrust leaves into its mouth. Elephants and lions live quite peaceably together. Only on rare occasions does a lion attack an elephant.

The giraffe is the tallest of all the animals. It uses its long neck to reach leaves on the tree tops. Its strong legs allow it to make a quick getaway, when it spots a hunting lion.

The zebras rest peacefully with the wildebeestes and gazelles. They are all alert to the approach of a hungry lion.

The rhinoceros has two big horns made of matted hair. The front horn is sometimes over one metre long. It uses its horn to root for food in the ground. When it charges an enemy, the rhino lowers its horn threateningly.

Flocks of pink-winged flamingoes line the shores of lakes. They search for shellfish and water plants in the mud flats, scooping them out with long curved beaks. They are ready to fly off at the sight of a lion.

In the heat of the day, the hippopotamus basks in rivers and shallow lakes. At night, it feeds on water plants and goes ashore to graze.

What is an extinct volcano?

Paricutin has not erupted for more than twenty years. It is a sleeping, or dormant, volcano. Although it may erupt again one day, it is quiet for the present.

The cone-shaped pile of dust and ash around the top of the vent has blown inwards, blocking the opening. The walls of the vent itself have collapsed under the weight of rocks and ash above them. The wind has smoothed away the sides of the volcano, and rounded them into a gentle, sloping hill. The top of the volcano now looks like a large, shallow dish.

When a volcano has ceased to erupt completely, it is called an extinct, or dead, volcano. Sometimes the top of its cone may collapse after a very violent explosion, causing the crater to become much wider, like a huge, shallow basin. Living things will begin to grow and flourish on the mountain slopes.

The rounded, shallow bowl of the crater is sheltered by its high, lava wall. Some craters slowly fill with rain water and become beautiful lakes. The lakes glow with strange colours from the minerals in the rocks which dissolve in the water.

In East Africa, the volcano Ngorongoro has been extinct for thousands of years. Thorny trees and grassland fill the crater and many animals graze there and bask in the sun.

Who was the Delphic Oracle?

The prophetess sat on a three-legged stool, chewing quietly and thoughtfully from a plate of laurel leaves. Grouped around her, silent and stern, stood the priests of the city of Delphi in Greece. As she muttered strange words, the priests listened carefully, trying hard to understand her meaning. They believed she was able to speak for the god Apollo.

The Greek rulers asked her advice on many important matters, and trusted her to tell exactly what was in store for them. Often her answers were vague, and her advice could either be taken to mean one thing, or quite the opposite. For many hundreds of years one prophetess after another held the important position of fortune-teller or oracle at Delphi.

How did Hyacinth die?

Apollo, the Greek sun god, enjoyed archery and other sports. He and his friend Hyacinth, a young athlete, often had contests to see who could throw a discus the furthest. One day Apollo had just made a powerful cast, when the West Wind began to blow. It blew the bronze discus so hard that it struck Hyacinth on the head and killed him instantly. Hyacinth's blood flowed onto the ground. From that spot sprang a deep-red or purplish flower, which is still called a hyacinth.

How can you become a jockey?

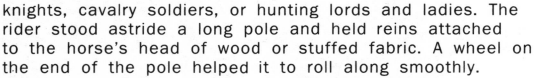

Children have always loved to pretend they are riding horses. Throughout history, they have mimicked chivalrous knights, cavalry soldiers, or hunting lords and ladies. The rider stood astride a long pole and held reins attached to the horse's head of wood or stuffed fabric. A wheel on the end of the pole helped it to roll along smoothly.

Two hundred years ago, children galloped and raced in parks, pulling behind them a carved, wooden horse on wheels. Many were painted in dapple grey spots with manes and tails made from real horse or cow hair. The saddle and the harness were often made from real leather.

The rocking horse was mounted on rockers, not wheels, and was an indoor toy. Early horses were shaped with round bottoms and gently tipped the child backwards and forwards. Later models were larger, gaily painted and rocked more wildly.

What rows the boat?

Clockmakers work with very delicate pieces of machinery. They put together clocks and watches using tiny springs, cogs and wheels. The metal parts are perfectly arranged and balanced so that one moving part sets another in motion.

In the eighteenth century, clockmakers began to experiment with clockwork toys, using simple bits of machinery to make the toys move. The simplest clockwork toy is powered by winding a spring tightly with a key. The spring is coiled around a metal bar, and this unwinds once the key is released or the toy is set down. Wheels and cogs attached to the bar are powered by this unwinding motion. They spin around driving the toys forward.

As well as clockwork animals and vehicles, there are many clockwork figures who dance, march or perform certain jobs when they are wound up. Musical boxes play simple tunes as tiny hammers inside strike coiled steel springs.

Where are bells hung?

Many years ago, the word belfry had nothing to do with bells. It once meant a tall tower built on wheels, that was pushed against the walls of a besieged town in order to storm it. Over the centuries the word has come to describe any tower where bells are hung. Belfries are usually part of a church. They are strong stone or wooden buildings. Flights of steps lead upwards to the top of the tower where heavy beams and rafters support the bells.

Some belltowers stand away from the church. One of the most famous is the Leaning Tower of Pisa in Italy. While this tower was being built about seven hundred years ago, it began to sink to one side. The tower still leans at an angle, and the top floor is constantly being weighted to prevent it falling over altogether.

Most of the large bells that you will hear are hung in a belfry. The bell is bolted to a strong iron bar called a headstock. The headstock and the bell are clamped to a wheel. At each pull of the bell rope, the wheel makes a half turn, bringing the bell into an upright, or handstroke position. Just before the bellringer makes the pull to sound the note, he tilts the bell in the opposite direction, or backstroke. The bell then swings round in a full circle, coming to rest in the handstroke position again.

Which is the largest bell?

The largest bell in the world is the Great Bell of Moscow, called the Tsar Kolokol. It was cast in 1733, and at that time people believed they could improve the note of the bell by throwing precious objects into the molten metal. Rich people threw in their jewels and coins when Kolokol was being cast. It did little good, for the bell was never hung. During the casting, the bell cracked and a large piece broke off. It is so huge that forty people can climb inside.

Who was Barbarossa?

The Barbary Corsairs had many famous leaders, including the desperate and fierce Barbarossa.

Barbarossa had seen his elder brother and his army of Corsairs hunted and killed by the Spanish. Barbarossa hated the Spanish and all the other Christian countries which had joined Spain in their battles against his brother. He took revenge for his brother's death by raiding coastal villages in France, Italy and Spain. His pirates looted, murdered, burned homes and carried off prisoners to sell as slaves.

Who was Blackbeard?

Edward Teach was another ferocious buccaneer. He had a long black beard, which was twisted into braids with ribbons and which hung down his chest like rats' tails. He was a terrifying sight with his weatherbeaten face and braided beard. To frighten his enemies, he put burning matches under his hat and firecrackers in his beard. His nickname was Blackbeard.

Blackbeard sailed for Jamaica to begin his life as a buccaneer, leaving his wife and children behind in London. This did not sadden him at all. During his lifetime Blackbeard had fourteen wives.

He raided ships off the coast of America and lived in great luxury. His crew was well-rewarded with shares of booty, especially rum. Blackbeard preferred a stronger drink. He mixed gunpowder in his rum.

Who has a diet of snails and who has a diet of fish?

Owls are night hunters. They often nest near farms where they hunt rats, mice and beetles that scurry around the barns. They are usually regarded as friends by the farmer. In the woods, owls catch voles, moths, snails, lizards and swallow them whole.

The owl's eyes are designed to see well in the dark. Huge round pupils pick up every small glimmer of light. Unlike other birds of prey, the owl also relies heavily on its hearing when it is hunting. Its large ear slits, hidden by flaps on the side of the head, pick up squeaks and faint sounds that a human ear cannot hear. The owl hunts by following these sounds. It glides silently after its prey and only swoops when the animal has been pinpointed exactly.

The osprey builds its nest on the shore of a lake or in a tall tree near the water's edge. The nest is made from branches woven with seaweed, driftwood and dead plants. Although ospreys are found throughout the world, very few of them breed in Great Britain. They used to be hunted because of the supposed damage they did to the trout and salmon industries, but now they are protected by law.

The osprey is a fish eater. It flies low over the surface of the lake, watching for any movement underwater. It hovers over the water, then plunges in, feet first, to grab the prey with its sharp talons. Sometimes the bird is pulled underwater, but its feathers are almost waterproof, and it soon rises to the surface, clutching its prey. The osprey's claws are covered with spiny pads which help it to grip the wriggling, slippery fish. It twists its four outer toes to grasp the fish around the middle.

Why are horseshoes lucky?

Devils and demons are powerful evil spirits. In Europe, devils were thought to have forked tails, pointed ears and cloven feet like goats' hooves. They often worked with witches to perform black magic. In the Middle Ages, one expert claimed that there were 1,758,064,176 devils at work in the world!

Ancient Persians, Hindus, Chinese and Japanese believed in demons of the underworld. In Japan the demons called Oni had red or green bodies with heads of oxen or horses. They drove fiery chariots to take away wicked people to the underworld. The gaki demons had huge bellies and were constantly tormented by hunger and thirst. They could take the shape of people or things to do their wicked deeds. Other demons were invisible but could be spotted by their singing, whistling and talking.

One of the most famous lucky charms is a horseshoe. A story tells how Saint Dunstan, who was a blacksmith, was visited by a strange-looking customer. The customer asked for a new horseshoe for his foot. Saint Dunstan recognized the shape of a split, or cloven, hoof. He immediately knew that this customer was the Devil.

He hammered on the horseshoe so roughly that the Devil screamed with pain and begged him to stop. But Saint Dunstan went on hammering mercilessly. He only stopped when the Devil promised that he would never enter a house with a horseshoe nailed over the door.

What was Atlantis?

Ancient legends describe a powerful country called Atlantis. High mountains surrounded a fertile plain where the people grew rich crops. They built cities with fine palaces and temples and dug canals for the water supply. But in time, the people of Atlantis grew greedy and spiteful. Suddenly a terrible disaster took place. The whole country disappeared forever beneath the sea. Many people have tried to find Atlantis. Some said it lay buried below the Atlantic Ocean or the North Sea. Today, archaeologists and historians believe that the lost world lies under the Aegean Sea, near the island of Thera. They have found remains of buildings and a palace containing ornaments and household objects.

It seems that the island of Thera, or Atlantis, was destroyed by volcanic eruptions, followed by earthquakes. The land was covered in ash and pumice. Later, great tidal waves swept over the island, and Atlantis disappeared forever.

Who was Vulcan?

Two thousand years ago, people did not know that rock and gas below the Earth's surface caused volcanoes to erupt. They were afraid of mountains that rumbled and exploded mysteriously. They believed that angry gods made the mountains erupt to punish them.

The Romans called their god of fire Vulcan. They believed that deep inside Mount Etna, on the island of Sicily, Vulcan heaped coals on his blacksmith's fire. This caused flames and sparks to leap up the chimney and through the mountain top. They thought that Vulcan forged the lightning in a thunderstorm. People imagined him hammering and beating the hot metal when they heard distant thunder. The word volcano comes from the name Vulcan.

Where does food come from?

The best crops are grown in rich, well-watered soil. Just as people and animals need food to grow strong and healthy, plants, too, need their own kind of food to grow and ripen.

Air contains a gas called carbon dioxide. Plants breathe in this gas through their leaves. They suck in the water from the soil through their roots. Sunlight helps the plant use the water and the carbon dioxide to grow.

A plant that stands in the sunlight is healthy. But a plant that is in the dark soon droops. Its leaves grow pale and withered.

People and animals rely on healthy crops to provide their food supply.

Cattle and sheep eat rich grass. They produce good milk and meat. People eat the meat and fruit and vegetables ripened by the sun. They drink milk and enjoy dairy foods such as cream, butter and cheese.

How do fish feed?

Vast numbers of tiny plants and animals float and drift in the sea. Many of them are so small that they can only be seen under a microscope. They are called plankton.

Animal plankton, or zooplankton, consists of small creatures such as grubs, sea urchins and unhatched fish eggs. Plant plankton, or phytoplankton, contains tiny plants and small pieces of seaweed. In the spring the phytoplankton blooms and spreads, turning the sea a rich green colour. Shoals of fish feed on the floating plankton as it drifts on the currents and tides. Scientists are developing ways to net plankton from the sea and to use it as food for land animals.

How do lions hunt?

Lions usually live together in a large family group called a pride. A pride may contain about fifteen lions, lionesses and cubs. The lionesses and cubs hunt, sleep and play together, while the lions look on, ready to protect them all fiercely.

When the pride goes hunting together, the work is shared. The pride stalks the prey, hidden by the undergrowth. One lioness leaves the pride and moves around into the wind. Her smell is carried to the grazing herd, who raise their heads in alarm. As the lioness rises, roaring, from the grass, they run quickly from her, driven forward into a waiting ambush of the other lions.

The lioness knows that towards dusk many animals go to the water hole or river to drink. Her sharp ears and eyes pick up the movement of a herd.

When she hunts alone, she approaches quietly, taking care that the wind is blowing towards her and carrying her scent away from the unsuspecting animals. She crawls silently forwards on her belly, crouching low in the grass or bushes. Suddenly she rushes. Her body arches and she springs onto the back of her prey, hauling it to the ground. In a flash, the lioness sinks her fangs into the animal's throat.

She drags away the carcass to a quiet spot where her family can eat its fill, the lion eating the most.

A lioness gives birth to cubs every two years or so. There may be two or three cubs in the litter. While young, the cubs feed from her milk. Sometimes a second lioness helps to rear and train the litter. At first, a cub's legs are weak. He rolls and staggers from side to side as he follows after his mother. The cubs tease the adult lions, nipping them with tiny teeth, or leaping on them with a squeaky growl. The rest of the time they sleep or gambol together.

The cubs are soon old enough to follow their mother on hunts. They copy her actions and when they are two years old, they will be able to hunt for themselves.

Who terrorized the China seas?

Chang Yih was a small hunchbacked Chinaman. He sailed on short pirate raids around the coast of China. He became very rich, and his fleet of stolen boats grew until he owned five hundred.

When Chang Yih was killed in a typhoon, his wife took charge of the fleet. She was even fiercer than her husband. Once she defeated a hundred ships belonging to the Emperor of China. Chang Yih's wife rewarded her pirates with silver for each victim's head that they brought her.

What are pieces of eight?

As soon as the Spanish discovered the treasure mines of Central and South America, they claimed them as their own. They built workshops near the mines which were called mints. Here they melted down the raw silver and gold and shaped them into large bars.

They moulded some of the gold and silver into coins. The largest silver coin was called an Eight Reale piece and was stamped with a figure 8. All the coins became known as pieces of eight. Pirates, who seized the Spanish treasure, used the coins all over the world. Eventually, countries stamped the coins with a picture of their king's head.

Many modern coins descend from the original Eight Reale piece.

What is white magic?

Primitive people understand little about the earth they live on or the world of outer space. They cannot explain why the sun moves across the sky, why thunder roars or why hurricanes blow, except as the work of supernatural spirits. They believe in spirits who control the sun, wind and rain and who live inside animals, plants and trees. Some of the spirits are good and helpful, while others are wicked and may cause harm or bring bad luck.

Since prehistoric times people have tried to influence or control these spirits and the mysterious world of the unknown by practising magic. There are two basic kinds of magic; black magic which is meant to cause harm and white magic which is helpful. People believed to be practising black magic have often been severely punished. White magic includes trying to foretell the future in different ways. This is a form of magic which is still very popular today.

What is a shaman?

A violent storm rages through the forest. In a clearing, the tribe gathers in front of the witchdoctor's hut, while he performs his tribal dances to frighten away the evil spirits of the storm.

As he leaps and twists, he chants spells in a low mumble or screeches curses at the sky. He wears a terrifying mask and his body is painted with powdered dyes and plant juices. He wears animal skins and bird feathers, and has the bones of dead animals in his hair and ears.

Many primitive tribes throughout the world choose one important person to perform the magic for his tribe. This man or woman may be called a witchdoctor, a medicine-man or shaman. They are often more powerful than the tribal chief, because the tribe believes they are in touch with supernatural spirits that control their lives.

How can you build a station?

Throughout the nineteenth century, brilliant scientists, engineers and electricians produced their inventions. When the Englishman George Stephenson introduced his famous steam engine Rocket in 1829, a new idea for a toy was born. Wooden models of this famous engine and its linked carriages could be pushed and pulled along the ground.

Toy steam engines, metal replicas of the Rocket and later engines, were also made. These engines were complicated pieces of machinery, and it took a great deal of time and tinkering to get them working. Each one was decorated with brass signs and shiny paintwork and had a small boiler which worked. A standard track size, called a gauge, was introduced so that several trains could circle the track at the same time.

Modern electric trains are even more complicated. Adults and children remain absorbed for hours, setting out the track, the stations, signal boxes, sidings and sheds, and enjoying the crisscross journeys of the model engines.

Toy bricks are simple shapes. They may be decorated on each face with colourful pictures or alphabet letters. when bricks of every shape and size are stacked and balanced on top of each other, they can become imaginary castles, lost cities or towering skyscrapers.

Small bricks that fit together can be made into complicated houses. Roof slates and chimneys, windows and doorframes help you to plan your construction like a real builder. Other kits provide metal shapes and angles which lock together using nuts and bolts and form intricate pieces of working machinery.

There are also construction toys for young aeroplane designers, shipbuilders or electricians. It takes a great deal of skill and care to put together a model glider made of balsa wood, for example. The pieces must be carefully glued together and balanced for smooth flight. There may be a small diesel engine or an electric receiver to mount on a radio controlled plane.

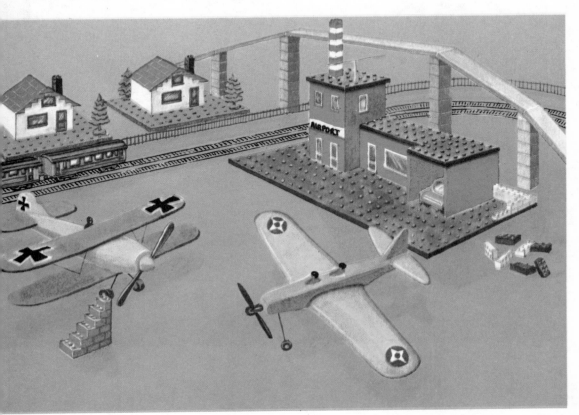

Which is the largest sea mammal?

Fish are creatures which are especially adapted to living in the sea. Fish breathe through small slits called gills which are at the sides of their heads. They are cold-blooded and their young hatch from eggs.

Mammals are animals which are better suited for living on land. They breathe air directly through their mouths and noses. They are warm-blooded. Their young are born alive and are not hatched from eggs. Young mammals feed on milk from their mothers' bodies.

There are a few mammals which live in the sea and rise to the surface to breathe from time to time. Their babies are born alive and suckle milk from their mothers' bodies. The seal, the walrus, the porpoise and the dolphin are all sea mammals, but the largest sea mammal is the whale.

Whales are hunted for their oil and meat. Beneath a whale's thick, tough skin is a layer of oily fat called blubber, which keeps the whale warm in cold seas. Blubber is made into oil which people burn in lamps and mix in their face creams, lipsticks, soaps and in some medicines. Whale meat feeds hungry people and dogs. Ground whale bones are used as crop fertilizer. Whale intestines contain a kind of wax which is used in making perfumes.

However, the whale has been hunted greedily for hundreds of years. There are so few whales left now that laws have been made to protect them. Once the sea around the South Pole teemed with the world's largest animals, Blue Whales. This huge whale can grow to more than thirty metres in length, which is even larger than the biggest dinosaur. Like the dinosaurs, there may soon be no Blue Whales left in the world.

How does the Fire Brigade fight a fire?

The correct name for a modern fire engine is an appliance. Various appliances are designed to carry different fire-fighting equipment. The appliance that races past your house to a fire nearby is probably a pump-escape or a pump.

Both appliances carry large tanks of water, with several taps on them. Each tap pumps water down a different hosepipe which is wound onto a large reel. On the tip of each hosepipe is a nozzle which controls the force of the water sending out a fine spray, or a fierce jet, depending on the size of the fire.

The Turntable Ladder reaches up to the top of high buildings. People climb down the ladder to escape the fire.

The Emergency Tender carries extra equipment such as oxygen breathing apparatus. At night it lights up the scene of the fire with searchlights.

Firemen throw ropes with hooks up to windows to grip the balconies and window ledges. Trapped people slide down the ropes to safety. Firemen lower injured people to the ground on stretchers. Special flame cutters melt through steel doors and bars to rescue anyone caught inside.

Fires in buildings along river banks or in seaports may be tackled by fireboats.

Why are lions and eagles painted on shields?

Throughout history, kings, princes, knights and noble lords have used a picture of a lion as a symbol of courage and high birth. They painted or engraved lions on their shields, flags and cloaks.

The Black Prince, a royal English knight, fixed a lion crest to his helmet. Another brave royal soldier, Richard I of England, became known as Richard the Lionheart. His shield and crest were decorated with three lions. He was a fierce, fearless fighter.

The lion is often seen as a 'supporter', holding up one or both sides of a shield. The Royal Arms, which is the emblem of the British Royal family, is supported by a lion and a unicorn.

For thousands of years conquering armies have followed an eagle flag, or standard, believing it would lead them to victory. In the first century A.D., the Romans tried to conquer the world. Each legion, or section of the Roman army, marched behind a standard on top of which was an eagle.

Many other kings and army leaders have since adopted the eagle as their symbol. Eagle banners were carried by knights to the Crusades. In the early nineteenth century Napoleon made the eagle the symbol of France.

In 1782 the Bald Eagle was adopted as the national emblem of the United States of America. The emblem, which is called the Great Seal, shows an eagle holding an olive branch, the symbol of peace, in its right talons and in its left talons are a bundle of arrows, the symbol of military power.

How did Queen Elizabeth I receive stolen goods?

Some men became pirates in search of adventure and glory rather than riches. They returned home after a voyage with a ship full of booty and presented it to their king or queen.

Francis Drake and his cousin John Hawkins were adventurers from England. They lived at the time of Queen Elizabeth I. England was at war with Spain, so Elizabeth encouraged her captains to rob Spanish ships. She supplied her men with good ships.

Each time her captains returned to English ports, they gave Queen Elizabeth shares of the Spanish booty. Both Francis Drake and John Hawkins were knighted, as a reward for their daring deeds.

Pirate captains, who plundered with the permission of their ruler, often carried Royal Letters to prove this. These pirates were called privateers. Their ships, also called privateers were very grand. Built by master craftsmen, they

were painted in bright colours and decorated with carvings and statues. Inside were elegant cabins which were comfortably furnished. Sir Francis Drake's ship, the *Golden Hind*, was a fine example of a privateer.

The crews were well trained and wore dashing uniforms. Privateers flew the flag of their country proudly.

How are vultures useful?

Vultures have ugly bald heads, often with a twisted and brightly coloured growth called a wattle, on their beaks. Some have blood red or bright yellow eyes and scraggy necks circled by ruffs of shaggy feathers.

Vultures are carrion eaters. The Condor, a large kind of vulture with a wingspan of three metres, feeds off dead cattle, sheep and rotting carcasses killed by other animals. They also feed off rubbish heaps.

Vultures have a reputation for being evil, unpleasant birds. Often they circle overhead or sit calmly waiting for their prey to die, before flocking in to rip its bones bare. In fact, vultures are useful because by clearing up rotting bodies, they help stop the spread of disease.